Live This Book

Live This Book

Abbie Hoffman's Philosophy for a
Free and Green America

By
Theodore L. Becker
and
Anthony L. Dodson

The Noble Press, Inc.

CHICAGO

Printed in the United States of America
Library of Congress Cataloging-in-Publication Data:

Becker, Theodore Lewis
   Live this Book : Abbie Hoffman's philosophy for a free and green America /
Theodore L. Becker and Anthony L. Dodson.
       p. cm.
   Includes bibliographical references and index.
      ISBN 0-9622683-9-9 (pbk.) : $11.95
      1. Hoffman, Abbie—Contributions in political science.   I. Title
JC251.H5372B43 1991
320.5'3'092—dc20   90-63430
                                                                  CIP

Printed on recycled paper

Noble Press books are available in bulk at discount prices. Single copies are available prepaid direct from the publisher:

Marketing Director
The Noble Press, Inc.
213 W. Institute Place, Suite 508
Chicago, Illinois 60610

To the Spirit of Abbie Hoffman:
"A Son of Liberty, Riding Through
the Night, Sounding the Alarm"

Contents

Foreword

A bbie was a prince of street politics, and no one played the role better. His excessive and outrageous acts stood out even in times that were marked by excess and outrage. He wrote, directed and played the '60s with shrewd calculation. An entire generation of American youth disillusioned by hypocrisy, racism and a war in Southeast Asia followed Abbie in body and spirit.

During the '80s Abbie carried his message of the dangers in the social, political and economic climate. His message of challenge and change was that this is a government of the rich by the rich for the rich and it shall taketh it from us. In the last decade of his life, his causes mirrored the changes and battles that we must face: the environment, racism and a foreign policy built on the interests of a few at the cost of many. His challenges went from a battle on the St. Lawrence River with the Army Corps of Engineers to a pump on the Delaware against Philadelphia Power and to the courtrooms of Northampton, where he met face to face with the CIA, exposing the myths and lies perpetrated on a public by a sold-out media that was on "bended knees" before the emperor himself, Ronald Reagan.

Abbie should always be remembered not by his death but for the legacy that he left to all of us. It was his spirit and "Revolution for the Hell of It" that took me and a lot of us out of an age of hypocrisy into the turbulent and wonderful "Age of Aquarius," through the cynicism of the '70s, into the greed of some in the '80s, into the obscurity of the greedy in the '90s and the dawning of a new spirit of revolution that will never die.

Jack Hoffman
15 April 1991, Patriots Day

Acknowledgments

We wish to acknowledge the encouragement, sustenance and assistance rendered to us by the following people whose many kindnesses and bemused forbearances were essential to the completion of this book:

Christa Slaton, for her humoring and helping her harried husband; conservative cousin Gary, for always being there; some close colleagues in the Department of Politcal Science at Auburn University (Tom Dickson, Gary Zuk, Mike Urban, Mike Budde and Bob Widell) who lent us moral and logistical support despite their doubts about our sanity; the secretarial staff at Auburn, who kept smiling despite rewrite, upon rewrite, upon rewrite; Rik Scarce, who put us onto The Noble Press; Mark Harris, our enthusiastic and personable editor, who made us appreciate the fact that publishing companies can be more like family than the federal government.

The locating of Abbie's writing was a task that required the help of many: we'd like to thank Dorothy Dodson (librarian extraordinaire), Steve and Rachel Dodson (book detectives), Jim and Mark Dodson, and the rest of the Dodson family for their sage advice and support. Also, without malice toward any we may have left out, thanks to Karen Consoli, Christock, the Dr. Robert Estock family, Kevin Cook, Vicki Lemarchand and "All Our Friends" on the Warrior River.

Introduction

Truth in Advertising

This is a book about Abbie Hoffman's political philosophy —
as we see it. It is not a book about THE political philosophy
of Abbie Hoffman. We know no one who could write such a
book, not even Mr. Hoffman himself, had he taken a crack at it.

Anyone who writes a lot about matters politic over such a
long period of time simply leaves clues to, and traces of, what
he or she thinks or feels about politics. Taken as a whole, there
are bound to be inconsistencies, contradictions, ambiguities
and changes of opinion. That's as true of Abbie Hoffman as it is
of Thomas Jefferson, Karl Marx or any political philosopher of
note or notoriety.

As we remark throughout this book, we believe that Jefferson stands out as one of the most eminent democratic theorists
of all time. But the same person who wrote about all men being
created equal and having the inalienable right of liberty was
himself a slaveholder. Moreover, Jefferson, the proponent of
small, weak government managed to engineer almost single-
handedly one of the most enormous real estate deals in history
(the Louisiana Purchase) when he was president of the United
States. Karl Marx, who wrote at length about the *theoretically*
fatal contradictions in capitalism, developed a philosophy that
rationalized socialist regimes with theoretically *and practically*
fatal contradictions.

Yes, we are sure that some skillful analysts who read what
follows could go to the basic source of this volume, the complete writings of Abbie Hoffman, and craft a dramatically different philosophical mosaic. We encourage them to do so. That
will reinforce the point we believe is crystal clear: Abbie Hoff-

man's writing about political matters is well worth taking seriously.

We also concede that there's a lot of "us" in this book. Any writer—poet, novelist, magazine columnist, political scientist, or newspaper reporter—has her or his own vantage point from which to behold the panorama of political life. We choose to see what attracts our glance, which is probably unlike that of the person standing beside us. Also, since no one can occupy the same physical space at the same time, no one can see quite the same thing as her or his neighbor.

What is more, the two authors of this book are not in precise agreement on the totality of Abbie Hoffman's life's work. We come from different backgrounds, succeeding generations and have had widely varying life experiences.

Each of us met Abbie Hoffman once in his lifetime. The senior author met him in New York City in late 1969. Becker was trying to develop a project for the American Civil Liberties Union in celebration of its fiftieth anniversary. It was to be a multimedia "event" at the Electric Circus in the East Village, and he thought that Abbie might be intrigued enough to lend a hand.

Hoffman had a wretched cold that day. Worse yet, he had been arrested the day before on what he claimed was a trumped-up charge, but was free on bail. He listened to the proposal but politely declined, saying that his plate was already too full. He wished the endeavor well and Becker went on his merry way.

The junior author, Dodson, met Hoffman on Halloween, 1985. At the time, Hoffman and his erstwhile compadre Jerry Rubin were barnstorming the country debating whether the idealism of the 1960s was alive and kicking in the United States of the 1980s. Their "Yuppie-Yippie Debate" had been invited to Mobile, Alabama, by Dodson, a student leader at the University of South Alabama at the time. He spent the day shepherding Hoffman around the campus and that gulfport city. For his effort, Hoffman gave Dodson a check for one million dollars. Although he claimed it was for "nothin," we like to think it was a pre-payment for taking the time and trouble to piece together one view of what Abbie Hoffman's political philosophy might be.

We want the reader to know, though, that we are in 100 percent accord on what we have chosen to include as the major elements, threads and conclusions of Hoffman's philosophy. We have eliminated or downplayed those bits, pieces and themes that we deem of lesser importance or that don't fit snugly into the more consistent and more mature patterns in Hoffman's thought that reveal themselves to us.

Additionally, we have highlighted what we think are the most quotable quotes in his books, what we call "sight bites." We think Hoffman's own words should stand out and speak for themselves. We've also emphasized certain quotes of other great political satirists and philosophers that are related in thought to Hoffman's (putting him in excellent company).

Abbie Hoffman was an impresario of political theatre, drama, comedy and philosophy. When he wrote, he sprinkled lustrous gems of political thought throughout his books and essays. We feel as though we have just finished prospecting for Hoffman's treasures and need to display our trove for the reader to see. He would approve of the "sight bite" method—even browsers in bookstores and libraries will get the message. For those who are strapped for cash, the "sight bites" are a way they can "steal" part of this book intellectually. If one wants the whole, rich philosophy, though, they'll have to read the entire book. For them, the "sight bites" will be Abbie's advertisement for himself.

So, for better or worse, this book is Becker and Dodson's view of *a* political philosophy of Abbie Hoffman. We hope each reader gets as much out of reading it as we got out of researching

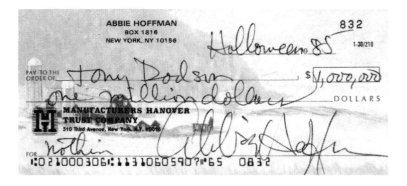

and writing it. We also hope it helps each reader get a better fix on her or his own homespun American political philosophy as the U.S.A. confronts the inevitable social, economic, ecological and political trials and tribulations of the 1990s. That's really why we wrote this book. We certainly don't intend to cash Abbie's check. Our intellectual debt to him exceeds his financial generosity to us.

Part One

Abbie Hoffman:
American Political Satirist, Theorist and Philosopher

Few familiar with the life of Abbie Hoffman, whether friend or not, consider him a political philosopher or believe that a major part of his life's work was political philosophy. The mission of this brief volume will be to demonstrate clearly, not only that Hoffman and his work centered around his political philosophy, but that his philosophy is an original and significant contribution to American political thought of the twentieth century. Moreover, as the title of this book is meant to convey, the political philosophy of Abbie Hoffman is not just a relic of the tempestuous 1960s. Rather, it is a living, rich testament and guide for all who yearn today for an environmentally and socially sound America in which individual freedom is still prized, protected, promoted and practiced.

To most who remember him, Hoffman's life was a patchwork of varied, sometimes contrasting qualities. He was colorful, but he had a coarse texture. He always seemed to be against something or someone, but he was in favor of having fun at the same time. A good deal of his adult life was spent in one kind of disguise or another, yet he always seemed ready to put everything he had on the line. He had a quick wit and a stiletto sharp sense of humor, yet he was deadly serious about achieving his goals. One thing few people accused him of being was a heavyweight thinker, but he wrote eight books in his abbreviated life. Abbie Hoffman a political philosopher? We believe he was.

Of course, Hoffman's main public persona, at least in his

early, most notorious years on the American political scene, was that of Clown Prince of the New Left—circa the late 1960s through the early 1970s—with his penchant for outlandish costumery and bizarre antics.

Some events that come to mind: (1) dumping a load of dollar bills onto the floor of the New York Stock Exchange to cause pandemonium, dramatize Wall Street's lust for money and interrupt business-as-usual, in Hoffman's words, "Showering money on the Wall Street brokers was the TV age version of driving the money changers from the temple."[1]

> Showering money on the Wall Street brokers was the TV age version of driving the money changers from the temple."
>
> *Abbie Hoffman*

(2) painting an obscene word on his forehead to insure he would *not* be on TV news that evening; (3) wearing a judge's robe into court during the Chicago Seven trial, removing it in front of the judge, throwing it to the floor and wiping his feet on it to telegraph his message of contempt and to tempt the judge to lose his composure (again); (4) nominating a swine for president of the United States in 1968, gluing wings on it and naming it "Pigasus." Do political philosophers behave like *that*?

Surely, Abbie Hoffman *was* a prankster. He clearly relished that image, but he saw it as vital to his role as an agent of democratic political, economic and social change in the United States. Hoffman was more than a mere practical jokester, he was a top flight political satirist in the best of that American tradition, one who self-consciously saw and used satire as a "political weapon."

Political Satire and Political Philosophy

Political satire is a time-honored way of poking fun at matters concerning government and politics. Such satire can come in the form of essays, songs, cartoons, books, poems, plays, or a new form of it explored by Hoffman—"guerrilla theater."

America has enjoyed its fair share of this generic art form, one that harks back to the ancient Greeks and has produced a goodly number of political satirists in this century alone, including Mark Twain, Will Rogers, Charlie Chaplin and, of course, Hoffman.

If a political satirist produces a large enough body of work in her or his career, it is bound to include some essential ingredients of a political philosophy. This is true of the work of all the above people. None of these famous satirists really thought of themselves as political philosophers and, with the exception of Hoffman, none of them really produced a comprehensive political philosophy. All of them, however, had two key elements of political philosophy in their political satire: (1) heavy criticism of American governmental policies and process and (2) an exposition of their own personal political values.

Since many people familiar with Hoffman's life would probably agree that there was a considerable amount of satire in his work, we think it is useful to show how he compares to Twain, Rogers and Chaplin.

Mark Twain: Self-Muted Critic

Mark Twain marbled his critical views of American political life with a broad vein of satire. In fact, it was he who popularized the comment that "there is no distinctly native American criminal class except Congress."[2]

It is noteworthy, though, that Mark Twain is best known and most fondly remembered by modern day Americans due to that part of his work which is almost totally barren of explicitly political content. Yet, Twain had strong feelings about politics and used his pen (which he said was "warmed-up in hell") as a rapier to cut to the heart of American social injustice and political hypocrisy and as a saber to slash at the facade of most patriotic hoopla so as to expose its demonic interior.

For example, Twain was particularly appalled by what he saw as the betrayal of the Filipino people in the late 1890s by the United States government, their alleged liberator from Spanish rule. Rather than protecting the Filipinos, the American military ended up waging a prolonged and bloody war against them. Twain's revenge for this and other wars of U.S. expansionism was to rewrite the *Battle Hymn of the Republic*, replacing pious rhetoric with gristly reality. His version started with:

> Mine eyes have seen the orgy of the launching of the Sword; He is searching out the hoardings where the stranger's wealth is stored . . . ; His lust is marching on.

And ended with:

> In a sordid slime harmonious, Greed was born in yonder ditch, With a longing in his bosom—and for others' goods an itch—As Christ died to make men holy, let men die to make us rich—Our god is marching on.[3]

Another example of this part of Twain's life is his highly regarded, but little known, *War Prayer*. It is a fable about an old

 There is no distinctly native American criminal class except Congress."

Mark Twain

man who goes to a church the day before local young volunteers are to leave for the battlefield. The preacher is praying for the Lord to help these young soldiers survive in battle and prevail over the despicable enemy. Then an old stranger—with long white hair and flowing robes—enters the church, walks up to the lectern and stands by the pastor's side. When the prayer concludes the old man announces that he is God's messenger and that God wants to make sure the congregation understands fully what it is truly asking God to do. The old man then restates the preacher's prayer:

> "O Lord, our God, help us tear their soldiers to bloody shreds with our shells; . . . help us to drown the thunder of the guns with the shrieks of their wounded, writhing in pain; help us to lay waste their humble homes with a hurricane of fire; help us to wring the hearts of their unoffending widows with unavailing grief; help us to turn them out roofless with their little children to wander unfriended the waste of their desolate land in rags and hunger and thirst . . . ."

The stranger finishes the *War Prayer* and then pauses.

"Ye have prayed it; if ye still desire it, speak!" . . . . It
was believed afterwards that the man was a lunatic, because there was no sense in what he said.[4]

However, some of Twain's most sardonic satire of the American
political scene, like the *Battle Hymn of the Republic* and the
War Prayer, were intentionally *not* published until *after* his
death. One reason for this was Twain's own admitted "coward-
ice," a personal reluctance to face the widespread and inevitable
criticism (and hatred) for his daring to tell the truth as he saw
it. He was at least, in part, a covert critic and a closet activist.
This in no way is meant to diminish Twain's courageous stands
on many social and political issues during his lifetime. It is only
mentioned to highlight Hoffman's willingness to publicize *all*
his views, to revel in the notoriety and to endure any and all the
painful consequences of his political satire and philosophy.

 Let us abolish policemen who carry clubs and
revolvers, and put in a squad of poets armed to
the teeth with poems on Spring and Love."
                                        Mark Twain

Twain's political and social commentary—even that published during his lifetime—left no doubt as to what his personal
political values were. He was an impassioned advocate of many
of the very same things that Abbie Hoffman stood for: freedom
of speech; a duty to avoid voting for either of two lesser candidates; and a fervent opposition to "the squalor of racial injustice,
the fraudulent distribution of wealth, and the exploitation of
their citizens by indifferent governments."[5] And, if we need any
further proof of how closely Twain's thinking about government
paralleled Hoffman's, remember that it was Twain himself who
said: "Let us abolish policemen who carry clubs and revolvers,
and put in a squad of poets armed to the teeth with poems on
Spring and Love."[6]

Will Rogers: Beloved Critic

Will Rogers led a charmed life despite persistently badgering the American political process and lampooning particular politicians of his day. Perhaps this was because of his persona as a lovable, wisecracking cowboy and/or his "aw, shucks" down-home style. Or maybe it had to do with his rosy outlook about the ordinary person and that he "never met a man [he] didn't like."

But from the start of his career as a rodeo and vaudeville star through his stints as a movie actor, newspaper columnist and general political curmudgeon, Rogers was constantly tweaking the nose of American politics and politicos—all of which gained him naught but increasing fame and popularity. In fact, he believed that nothing was safe from his acid tongue no matter how grave the problem. His view was "the more serious the situation the better they (Americans) laughed *if you happened to hit the right angle to it.*"[7]

All this gave him a great deal of power, a "hold" on the American public, but it was one he never personally desired to convert into actual political power. In 1924, he was nominated for President at the Democratic Convention and in 1928 he was involved in a parody of a political movement called the "Anti-Bunk Party." But when he was seriously approached by some financial backers to run for the U.S. Senate from California, he made the following public offer: "If you see or hear of anybody proposing my name for any political office . . . maim (him) and send me the bill."[8]

Nevertheless, after years of writing columns and a few books, a body of political thought emerged from this "cowboy philosopher" (as he billed himself). What it amounted to, though, was more of a collage of witty skepticism about a political system that tilted strongly in favor of the rich and as strongly against the poor, a system that was run by a breed of politicians that was at best inconsistent and hypocritical and at worst totally disingenuous and dishonest. Or, as Rogers once ad-libbed (as though he were alive in 1991 witnessing the continuing Savings and Loan Crisis): "See where Congress passed a 2 billion-dollar bill to relieve bankers' mistakes and lend to new industries. You can always count on us helping those who have lost part of their fortune, but our whole history records nary a case where the loan was for a man who had absolutely nothing."[9] In addition, according to one of his biographers, "In thus urging the case against domination of the country by the interests, Rogers as the American democrat was becoming co-essential with the dream of freedom. He merged himself with that vision, too, by defending in his commentary the freedom of press, speech and religion."[10]

 See where Congress passed a 2 billion-dollar bill to relieve bankers' mistakes and lend to new industries. You can always count on us helping those who have lost part of their fortune, but our whole history records nary a case where the loan was for a man who had absolutely nothing."

Will Rogers

These general themes, as we shall see, are precisely the same as Abbie Hoffman's. Rogers' written work contains a similar amount of negative description and many of the same positive American political values as Hoffman's. What Rogers' work lacks, as does Twain's, is any exhortation towards radical change in the system, a call that is essential to a fully formed political philosophy. It is not surprising then that those in power during Rogers' time hobnobbed with this darling of the newspapers, radio and movies while those of Hoffman's time shunned and persecuted him. Rogers was a clever satirizer who spoke to the underlying dissatisfaction most Americans felt about American politics at that time—but he said and did nothing about altering that system. Hoffman was a political philosopher who lived his criticism and his view of how to challenge and restructure the system he mocked. Will Rogers was a social safety valve. Abbie Hoffman was a political threat.

Charlie Chaplin: Self-Exiled Critic

Although a British citizen, Charlie Chaplin practiced most of his political and social satire in the United States, basing a great deal of it on what he experienced while in America. It is somewhat difficult to *write* about the content of his political satire since a substantial part of it was visual and non-verbal — in silent motion pictures. Moreover, there is much controversy over exactly what political messages and values his films were meant to transmit.

According to his critics, Chaplin was a communist, a socialist or, at best, a sympathizer to these immoral and inept ideologies. Thus, from their point of view, his characterizations added up to an indictment of righteous American capitalism and a favorable view of Russian wrongheaded communism.

According to Chaplin himself and many artistic critics and academics, Chaplin's satire had a far broader social content than any one particular political/economic ideology. Like Hoffman, his major complaints were against the dehumanization and sausagization of individuals in modern industrial society, particularly by what he often called the "machinery." He was artistically sympathetic to the average person in society trying to survive the greed of those who owned those monstrous tools and assembly lines, whom he called "the idle class" in one of his films.

The little person was also innocent cannon fodder for military machines. Chaplin — like Twain before him and Hoffman thereafter — was indignant about nations mobilizing, wounding and annihilating citizens under a false morality and ersatz patriotism that was mostly a cover for economic reasons ("expanded industry and new jobs"). In such military campaigns, the rich see little action and gain bushels of money. The poor see a lot of dying and misery and gain parcels of medals and horrible memories. As Chaplin put it in his autobiography: "Those that were not killed or wounded did not escape, for many were left with deformed minds. Like a minotaur, war had gobbled up the youth, leaving cynical men to survive. But we soon forget and glamorize war with popular Tin Pan Alley ditties: 'How're you going to keep them down on the farm, after they've seen Paree—' "[11]

However, Chaplin was not a total pacifist (though he referred to himself as a "peacemonger"). Indeed, prior to Pearl Harbor he spoke out frequently in favor of the United States getting more involved in the Second World War against the Nazis.

 Those that were not killed or wounded did not escape, for many were left with deformed minds. Like a minotaur, war had gobbled up the youth, leaving cynical men to survive. But we soon forget and glamorize war with popular Tin Pan Alley ditties: 'How're you going to keep them down on the farm, after they've seen Paree—' "

Charlie Chaplin

Chaplin's hatred of Hitlerism far superceded his dislike of its Anti-Semitism. Another "machine" he loathed was that of fascism in any form, including its manifestations in the U.S. He ran afoul of virulent anti-communism and rabid nationalism in the U.S. in the 1940s and 1950s, which cast him as an enemy. The news media, along with a variety of political and religious organizations (Catholic War Veterans, the American Legion), slowly turned against him. Finally he became the target of several government agencies (the Department of Justice, the House Un-American Activities Committee, and the U.S. Immigration Service).

Chaplin admitted he had friends who were communists. He had made many speeches during the Second World War that lauded the Soviet struggle against the Germans. But it was his social satire and his resistance to the forces of thought control that proved his undoing. For Chaplin was hardly a political activist. He insisted, and it was never proved otherwise, that he had never joined any political organizations in his lifetime— much less subversive ones. In fact, he, like Will Rogers, was a fellow traveler mainly of the rich and famous—fraternizing and socializing with them in their palaces, yachts and country clubs.

It was what he *said* in his movies, what captured the minds and hearts of millions around the world, that caused his downfall in America. One does not have to be a Marxist, a socialist or a communist to believe, as Chaplin did, that: "The accumulating complexities of modern life, the kinetic invasion of the twentieth century, find the individual hemmed in by gigantic institutions that threaten from all sides, politically, scientifically and economically. We are becoming the victims of soul-conditioning, of sanctions and permits."[12]

> The accumulating complexities of modern life, the kinetic invasion of the twentieth century, find the individual hemmed in by gigantic institutions that threaten from all sides, politically, scientifically and economically. We are becoming the victims of soul-conditioning, of sanctions and permits."
>
> *Charlie Chaplin*

Chaplin's objects of derision were America's "moral pomposity," its "powerful cliques and invisible government." This is compatible with the view of Jan and Cora Gordon, two analysts of his work in the 1930s, who observed that " . . . the *bourgeoisie* instinctively repudiate him. He stands for something that denies the whole of their collective philosophy. He proclaims the importance of subtle spiritual values that may lie behind failure . . . . The members of the great *bourgeoisie* may be amused at Charlie in spite of themselves, but there is something in him repugnant to them." [13] In his own mind's eye, he became persecuted and prosecuted not because he was a communist, socialist or believer of any labelled ideology, but, instead, because he was Charlie Chaplin, true to his own individual belief system. Or as he put it: "My prodigious sin was, and still is, being a nonconformist."[14]

Unlike Twain and Rogers, Chaplin fell out of favor in a country that had adored and lauded his artistic work. Like

Twain and Rogers, he was fond of hobnobbing with the American economic and political elite of his time. Unlike Twain and Rogers, he became an anathema and suffered serious personal consequences for his audacity and individual social beliefs. Thus, his fate was more like Abbie Hoffman's. Chaplin became hated and hounded even though, unlike Hoffman, he never advocated any comprehensive changes in American policies or its form of government and never acted out any of his negativity towards the system. Perhaps he eventually became hated because

 My prodigious sin was, and still is, being a nonconformist."

Charlie Chaplin

he was a foreigner (never obtaining U.S. citizenship). It surely wasn't that he had written and/or lived out any kind of political ideology or philosophy. Like Hoffman, governmental harassment led Chaplin to self-exile. Unlike Hoffman, his was relatively apolitical and permanent.

Abbie Hoffman made public ridicule an important part of his political philosophy of action and social change. This made him unique as a political satirist and an unusual political activist. It was also a major contribution that Hoffman made to modern American political theory.

Political Theory and Political Philosophy

So Hoffman—like Twain, Rogers and Chaplin—mixed a large portion of sarcasm into his critique of the American political scene. He was equally clear in his allegiance to key American political values which had been embraced and expounded by his predecessors in contemporary American political satire, e.g., the importance of individual freedom in American democracy. But, unlike the others, Hoffman took a further intellectual step toward being a political philosopher. He was a political theorist—and an extraordinarily good one.

Political theory is that kind of intellectual activity whereby one thinks about or imagines general relationships between two or more aspects of reality, at least one of which is political in na-

ture. So, if we say that there is less personal freedom in a socialist society than in a capitalist country, then we have made
a political theoretical statement. Put another way, we are saying
that almost all nations we classify as socialist will score lower
on a measuring device that calibrates individual liberty than
will most (if not all) nations that we categorize as capitalist. The
abstract relationship we are theorizing about is between types
of political economy and degrees of personal liberty. That's pure
political theory.

Abbie Hoffman did a lot of abstract thinking in his books,
but he also decided *how* to accomplish certain political objec-
tives on the basis of more tactical theorizing. For example, he
theorized that there was a relationship between how one
presented oneself to the mass media and whether one could get
"free media" exposure, i.e., not have to pay the TV station to
carry one's political message. Then he tested his theory time and
time again in reality. He was what might be called an "action
theorist," that is, he developed political theories, particularly
regarding the interface of the electronic media and politics, and
personally experimented with them by acting them out or setting the stage for others to do so.

In this regard, all modern day political consultants are
political theorists too. They get paid to understand the relationships between various types of political ploys and the impact
these will have on potential and actual voters. They calculate
what kinds of "photo opportunities" will play well on TV, what
kinds of advertising will appeal to which demographic groups,
and the like. Then they test them in a variety of elections, tabu-
late and record the results, and develop their own theories for
which they charge a hefty price to implement. Hoffman did
much the same, but for causes instead of candidates. He didn't
consider financial remuneration the major reward for his ideas.
Challenging and changing "the system" was what he was all
about—and this is where the political theorist and political philosopher part company.

All political theorists are *not* political philosophers, but all
political philosophers *are* political theorists. This is just another way of saying that political philosophers do exactly the
same thing that political theorists do—except they do some-

thing else too. The difference is that political philosophy adds an important ingredient to the work: a strong commitment to a set of values and preferences that motivate the thinker in her or his work. What is more, these views about the way the world *should be* are made quite clear. They are not denied or fudged. They are trumpeted page after page.

Many modern political theorists claim their work is "objective" and "value-free." That, however, is not possible. We all have our biases which guide our work and influence what we see and how we interpret what we see. There is a long-standing debate among political scientists about this. Many self-styled "empirical political theorists" insist that their work is purely scientific, that there are no morals or personal preferences involved in their work. This claim, however, is either fanciful or a self-delusion. Even the purest natural scientists are dominated by their value systems: cancer researchers are not dispassionate, neutral researchers. They hate malignant growth and passionately hope to arrest it.

The key difference between political theory and political philosophy, then, is not whether there are values that guide and influence the thinking and research process. What distinguishes the two is whether these values are subtle, implied or even camouflaged, or whether they are openly and manifestly integrated throughout the thought process.

Besides being an excellent political theorist—as we have stated earlier—Hoffman parades his passion, his compassion, his mores, his choices and his values throughout his written work. They are carefully and repeatedly weaved into his writing. They are the *raison d'etre* of his literary life. This is what transforms his lifework into political philosophy.

Underrating Political Philosophy in the USA

When we think of political philosophers, though, who comes to mind? To the average person, or to those with formal, higher education, Plato, Aristotle, Cicero, St. Thomas Aquinas, Rousseau, Hobbes, Locke, Bentham, Madison, Jefferson, Marx, and Lenin, fall into that exclusive club. There is not a political satirist in the lot.

Political philosophy is generally thought to be contained

only in lengthy, dull, obtuse books—extremely difficult to read and even harder to understand. As good fortune would have it, the common wisdom goes, such subject matter is the singular preserve of certain college-level political science courses and can even be avoided as electives in university philosophy departments.

It is thought that those who study this material are either majors in these fields, crashing bores, would-be politicians and/or sadomasochists. It is also widely believed that political philosophy is of meager to no relevance once a final exam has been passed. Political philosophy, in other words, is not something for which most parents happily or proudly pay tuition. But they forgive the transgression once their offspring is working on her or his law degree or Master's in Business Administration.

The truth is that, despite the common aversion to it, political philosophy effects most people much more than they dare admit.

Let's compare political and religious philosophy in American life. Most Americans are conversant in, if not well acquainted with, the tenets and principles of their personal theological texts. They study them. They seek guidance and consolation in them in their hours of greatest need. They make pilgrimages to houses of worship and dote on explanations. They make overt and private efforts to practice them. They heed discussions about dissent within their own sects. But American *political* philosophy, even that which underlies the very government that influences almost every aspect of their daily lives, is not something they want to take consciously and conscientiously to heart and mind.

Whereas many Americans can quote the 23rd Psalm, few have even heard of Federalist Paper No. 10. Whereas almost any American can accept the fact that there are numerous dissenters to their own religious beliefs and are willing to concede (albeit begrudgingly) that freedom of religion is and should be protected (part of American political philosophy), few can understand or tolerate dissent from the American political system— even though this dissent is equally protected by freedom of speech, press and thought (another cardinal principle of American political philosophy.)

When Americans debate politics at all, it is usually at the policy level. What should be the limits on abortion, if any? Should military force be used in the [fill in the current] crisis"? What social programs should be cut so Congress can balance the budget? These are the kinds of things that American citizens — those precious few who still pay attention to national politics — ponder in the daily course of events.

Much fewer debate such weighty matters as: How can one get a fair trial in a political case? What are the ways we can minimize the influence of the military-industrial complex on our foreign policy? How can people best act and/or mobilize to protect their personal freedoms and their natural environment? What are useful strategies and tactics for wresting the power of the mass media from the hands of the same power elite that control the economy and the government? These queries address political power, structure and strategy. They are political philosophical matters and are central to the written work of Abbie Hoffman. The answers he provides are meant to help put the power to answer policy questions back into the hands of the American people.

One way he tries to do that is to write his political philosophy in an interesting and humorous style, making it accessible and even appealing to the average citizen. Most philosophers or philosophy professors are elitists who do not have a truly democratic outlook. Thus, they use a jargon that discourages and excludes an average readership. They disparage an easily read and entertaining treatise as being beneath philosophy when, in truth, it's a philosophy with a higher purpose and broader appeal.

The Structure of Hoffman's Philosophy

As we have noted before, comprehensive political philosophies routinely pretend to provide an accurate, unbiased description of the deeper political realities by which humanity lives. They may be society specific, time specific, or they may lay claim to portraying the most universal and infinite truths.

Description of the Problem: Pictures of Dorian Gray

Without exception, at least part of that vision is decidedly unpleasant. Political philosophers are not adverse to extremely negative depictions of what they want their readers to see and/or believe. Portraits of political life to political philosophers often are pictures of an aged Dorian Gray—wrinkles, warts, scars, pock marks, bleeding sores. After all, if things weren't so bad, who would want to read a political philosophy?

For example, to Thomas Hobbes, the lives of primitive humanity were "solitary, poor, nasty, brutish and short," and this caused them to "invade, and destroy one another."[15] The Founding Fathers of the American Constitution based their intricate governmental structures and strictures on their unshakable faith in the eternal avarice and exclusively self-serving routines of *all* people. Karl Marx's evaluation of the status of laborers under the capitalistic yolk was that they were exploited, manipulated and chained to misery.

Similarly, the foundation of Hoffman's philosophic writing is a chilling account of political life in modern day America. One need not agree that his view is totally or even partially correct. What is important, for this analysis, is that it must be understood that his view of a harsh political landscape is absolutely true, *from his perspective*. Whether or not one cares to read more depends on the degree that the reader agrees with Hoffman's portrait of society. The closer the philosopher's negative view conforms to the reader's, the more likely the latter will want to discover what the philosopher thinks are the causes of this sorrowful situation.

Causes and The Bad Guys

Since all political philosophies are also political theories, merely describing the inhospitable or hostile world in which we live is not nearly enough. Relationships must be established. There must be reasons. Malice thrives: it may be innate in human nature, it may inhere in our form of government, it may lurk in who owns the mode of production, or it may be a residue of our cultural ignorance or the result of some technological imperative.

Abbie Hoffman has a wide array of bad guys in his philosophy. As we will see, there is not too much in his theory of what factors are behind America's political malaise that is new. In addition, he draws some of his analysis from other major philosophers. It is a mixture of mostly classical themes with some new perspectives as to whom and what are to blame for the present day American predicament—as he sees it. There are fools who do stupid things. There are villains who do evil things. There is cause. There is effect. But while there are insidious forces of history at work, there are also positive energies of history at play. Here is where Hoffman adds his most innovative contributions to modern American political philosophy.

Visions of a Better Place

One can tell that s/he is dealing with a political philosophy not only because it soon becomes apparent what the writer deprecates, disdains, despises or detests, but also because it will become equally clear as to how the writer hopes to help the world become a better place. Most political philosophies, then, are characterized by the fact that they construct a new polity, one which will be fairer, more just, more effective and durable.

To Adam Smith, Utopia-on-Earth was a wealthy, capitalist-driven nation state. Karl Marx's vision was that paradise on this planet would be reached when a "classless society" emerged, leading to "the withering away of the state." James Madison's ideal government was an intricately balanced, well-defined mechanism where power was divided and government so at odds with itself that it could accomplish little—and slowly at that.

Hoffman did not have an elaborate image of what government would look like in the dim, distant future—but he did have some general concepts and a few concrete ideas. He himself admitted that he was no "deep thinker" and mistakenly anointed himself as "anti-intellectual." Actually, he was more oriented towards thinking about future policies and political processes than he was towards visions of fixed forms of governance. He had some trouble in identifying himself in terms of a consistent, recognizable, political philosophical position. Sometimes he called himself a "socialist." Sometimes he sounded like an "anarchist." Many saw him as a prophet of the "New Left."

He was, though, an apostle of disestablishmentarianism (someone who advocates perpetual and radical alteration of the established forms and processes of power). But he was not merely negative. He saw a great need for improvement in the output of the political system, changes best characterized as "new age" or "transformational." He knew a lot about how to galvanize people into an active force to manipulate the system and, thus, vary its policies.

Way(s) To Go: American Political Existentialism

It was in his prescription of how to help alter a modern, technological, hierarchically-structured, elected "representative" system that Hoffman excelled as a political philosopher. Yes, he was a tactician, but he was something more, too. In the main, he was an abstract philosopher of modern political activism. He had an original perspective on politics as individual, internally personalized action, both inside and outside "the system."

If Existentialism is not a philosophy of life, then Abbie Hoffman was not a political philosopher, and his accumulated writings do not amount to a political philosophy. Modern Existential philosophy has been a response to the challenge of defining a meaningful, ethical life in a world where ultimate morality and social values are open to doubt or reduced to "absurdity." It was a philosophy that tried to encourage or justify individual "being" and personal significance in relationship to a cosmic mirror reflecting only "nothingness."

In like fashion, the essence of Hoffman's philosophy treats the problem of how to generate meaningful individual political action: how to get people to act, in the face of seemingly overwhelming odds, against a dominating, immoral and/or amoral authority. This intimidating and highly manipulative power fosters a sense of abject helplessness in people that discourages participation in politics, and, in fact, actually is designed to encourage a massive, dispirited exodus from active participation in the system. It was Hoffman's goal to develop a philosophy of political engagement, one that would get citizens to rebel against that power, to define their own personal rights and lives in terms of their own personal political agendas and activities. This objective is certainly not novel in political philosophy, nor is it of modern origin. The political philosophy of some ancient Greeks—particularly during the Golden Age of Pericles' Athens—was a paean to the marriage of individual, personal existence to the public and political life. One could not truly "Be" unless one was actively involved in the pursuit of civic life. In the words of Pericles himself: "We do not say that a man who takes no interest in politics is a man who minds his own business; we say that he has no business at all."[16]

Hoffman's own challenge, though, was to motivate and organize political action in a nominally democratic system which, from his viewpoint, cleverly subverted and/or ruthlessly threatened the incentive for public action by most citizens. His challenge also included the solution of the dilemma of rousing people to take major risks in a society that conditions its populace into the overriding value of personal, materialistic hedonism. Finally, and most importantly, Hoffman knew he had to educate and convince individuals to behave effectively in a system in which power comes less from the barrel of a gun than it does from the lens of a television camera. These are foci in his thoughts on the way(s) the American people have to go to overcome the serious obstacles on their path to a better and sustainable public and private life in the future.

The Relevance of the 1960s Counterculture to a Philosophy for the 1990s

So what has a political philosophy based substantially on the experiences of such a strange and extraordinary period like the 1960s and 1970s got to do with the equally novel problems that American society will face in the 1990s and beyond?

First, it must be said that *all* political philosophies are based, at least in large part, on the particular political facts of their time. They are mostly rooted in the peculiar cultural and intellectual developments of the moment. However, the underlying causes of the political diseases that compel people to rebel and philosophers to philosophize remain generally the same from nation to nation and time to time.

In all cases of extreme political turmoil, we find massive numbers of citizens dissatisfied with the way they are being ruled, leaders of dissident groups being singled out for harsh treatment, overwhelming numbers of people taking to the streets sooner or later against their government and anti-government political literature. In this century alone, we discover these patterns in, to name a few, the Russian Revolution; the development of the American labor movement; the counter-culture movements in the United States, France, Germany, Mexico and Japan in the 1960s; the overthrow of the Shah of Iran; the overthrow of the Marcos regime in the Philippines; the overthrow of communist regimes in Poland, Hungary and East Germany in the late 1980s and, someday, perhaps in the Soviet Union.

Extreme political turmoil also existed back in colonial America. According to a highly regarded and widely adopted current American government college text: "Within five months after the incident in Boston [the Boston Tea Party], the [British] House of Commons passed a series of acts that closed the port of Boston to commerce, changed the provincial government of Massachusetts, provided for the removal of accused persons to England for trial, and most important, restricted movement to the West—further alienating the Southern planters who de-pended upon access to new western lands. These acts of retalia-tion confirmed the worst criticisms of England and helped radicalize Americans."[17]

Thus, a small group of patriots asked Thomas Jefferson to draft a political philosophical statement to sum up the many wrongs committed by the British government against the American colonists and to provide some general principles that would guide people on a proper course of revolution against that government.

Jefferson worked hard to incorporate, within one very brief document, the major ingredients of a political philosophy. Thus, his *Declaration of Independence* included: (1) a section on what wrongdoings the English perpetrated against the colonists: "Obstruct[ing] the Administration of Justice," "impos-ing taxes on us without our Consent," "destroy[ing] the lives of our people"; (2) a statement of political philosophical values

and truths: "all men are created equal," "Governments . . .
deriv[e] their just powers from the consent of the governed"; (3)
and visions of appropriate future political action: "whenever
any Form of Government becomes destructive of these ends, it
is the Right of the People to alter or to abolish it, and to institute
new Government . . . ."
Although Jefferson's masterpiece of political philosophy
was based on the foul deeds committed by the King of England
against his "subjects" in the New World, no one can deny the
universality of his philosophy. And so it is with all political
philosophies . . . Abbie Hoffman's included.

Second, although it cannot be proven scientifically, there
have been a number of keen observers through time who have
noticed at least one remarkable pattern in American history, a
repetition of political upheavals in somewhat regular periods of
time. Some call them "cycles," some call them "spirals," others
characterize them as "alternations." There are also slight differences in the number of years by which these historians calibrate
these periods of change. However, despite significant differences in how these patterns are described and timed, there is an
even more amazing similarity in what these interpreters of history say about them.

In 1986, Theodore L. Becker put it like this: "Around the
turn of the century, the Progressive Movement flourished as a
reaction to corporate corruption of the democratic process. It
produced an emphasis on direct democracy, citizen initiatives
and anti-trust laws. Fifteen years or so later, American politics
shifted from an anti-establishment bias to a reaction against foreign radicals, i.e., the 'Red Scare' of the early 1920s. About fifteen years later, during the Great Depression, a new anti-
establishment movement waxed: The New Deal and the advent
of welfare capitalism. This movement was followed, approxi-
mately fifteen years later, by the McCarthy Era, a time of extreme conservatism. Fifteen years subsequent to that, America
found itself in the middle of a strongly anti-establishment
'generation gap,' the women's liberation movement, and the
'counterculture.' And after another fifteen years had passed,
Ronald Reagan was ensconced in the White House as the apostle
of a new conservatism. This does not mean that the late 1990s,

at the threshold of the Third Millennium, will witness a new anti-establishment movement reaching a new peak. But it may."[18]

In Becker's analysis, there are several keystones: (1) the cycle is one of anti-establishment vs. pro-establishment; (2) there is slow, incremental change in favor of more and stronger democracy; (3) the ebb is fifteen years and the flow is fifteen years, with a total of thirty for the entire span; (4) it is not certain that this democratic spiral will continue in the future, but it is likely.

At roughly the same time Becker published his observation, Arthur M. Schlesinger, Jr., was writing his book *The Cycles of American History*.[19] In Schlesinger's view, those who have detected such "alternations" in American history have been "wise men." To bolster his point, he notes that Ralph Waldo Emerson described a struggle between the parties of "Conservatism" and "Innovation" that wavers back and forth throughout American history. Some fifty years after Emerson, the great American historian Henry Adams saw a slightly different cycle, a tension between, in Schlesinger's words, "the centralization and diffusion of national energy."[20]

Schlesinger notes that he inherited "an alternative interpretation of this cyclical phenomenon from my father, who defined the swing between conservatism and liberalism, between periods of concern for the rights of the few and periods of concern for the wrongs of the many."[21]

He believes, as do we, that there will be a major swing from the conservative, private interest period of the 1980s toward a "public purpose" in the 1990s, "a change comparable to those bursts of innovation and reform that followed the accessions to office of Theodore Roosevelt in 1901, of Franklin Roosevelt in 1933 and of John Kennedy in 1961."[22]

This "public purpose" may become apparent in the near future, possibly as early as 1992 or 1996—in the event of the loss of the presidency by the Republicans. The social, economic, ecological and political problems will then have become so severe that the nation will be begging for new directions, a new genus of leaders, and new approaches—perhaps a dramatic political transformation.

It will be at that moment that a truly American political philosophy — one rooted in contemporary problems, one that understands the role of electronic media in politics, one that preaches the importance of the individual citizen in political change, one that truly grasps the significance of human liberty and direct democracy — will become critically important. What is more, being sensitive to contemporary and future crises, Hoffman's philosophy incorporates the importance of a sound physical environment into its text. The next step in American democracy must connect the polity to its physical environment, and Hoffman's philosophy helps address that task.

Reading Hoffman is easy and educational. Living his philosophy will be hard. The rest of this work will take us through the easy part. The hard part will then be up to us and you.

Part Two

Elements of Hoffman's Philosophy:
What's Wrong with America

The Malady and the Virus

Abbie Hoffman's views on his country's social, economic and political faults were and are hardly revelations to America's eyes and ears. Similar viewpoints can be located everywhere on the spectrum of critiques from the extreme right, to the extreme left, to newly emerging ways of looking at breakdowns in American society and what can be done to repair them. In Hoffman's works, one finds elements of Libertarian philosophy, Marxism and neo-Marxism, New Age thinking and Green ideology.

Consistent with the Libertarian Right, there was his visceral aversion to increasing governmental interference with individual liberty and coordinated governmental assaults on the "right to privacy." With the Left, he agonized over what he saw as increasing social injustice in the United States—as well as over a decreasing equality of opportunity. In collaboration with New Agers, Hoffman was a complaining witness about how "the system" is undermining the values of community and spirituality in America. In sympathy with Greens and ecologists, he fretted over and fought to stop the rapid erosion of the environment and its serious consequences for the present and future of the U.S.A.

Although Hoffman was not a certified researcher or scholar, during his lives as undergraduate student, graduate student and hyper-activist, he ran across writings and lectures of numerous celebrated academicians and political commentators of the time that contained much data, opinion and theory on America's contemporary problems. Although he did not refer to or cite any professional authorities on this subject in his writings, there can be little doubt that his outlook on socio-political disintegration in the United States in the twentieth century was informed and formed to some degree—directly and/or indirectly—by some of the more prominent figures in this coterie of critics.

For example, as will be seen shortly, Hoffman understood and stated—as a serious student of the American polity—that a minuscule clique of people tend to dominate the major public and private centers and institutions of power, a group that strongly resembles what C. Wright Mills and others have dubbed "the power elite."[1] He realized that they also owned a vastly disproportionate share of the wealth of the nation, and as detailed by G. William Domhoff,[2] they mingle, merge and intermarry customarily.

Hoffman was in good company in his view that as a consequence of this pooling of power in the hands of such a tight-knit and affluent cabal the rich actually get richer and the poor truly do get poorer. Scholars from the left, like Edward Greenberg[3] and from the right, like Kevin Phillips,[4] have amassed titanic stacks of evidence to prove, well beyond a reasonable doubt, that this trend has not only held throughout the twentieth century in the United States, but shifted into overdrive during the two Reagan Administrations, circa 1980–88, aptly baptized the Decade of Greed.

During his lifetime as a student of American politics, Hoffman was also privy to incipient theories on the intensive growth and extensive power of American corporate leviathans and their pervasive incursion into almost every nook and cranny of American life. Just as the craggy landscape of skyscrapers dwarfs pedestrians in every modern American city, so does the corporate hierarchical structure threaten to crush individual creativity and the freedom of its workers and clientele. Post-World War II books like David Riesman's The Lonely Crowd[5] and William H. Whyte's The Organization Man[6] minted phrases to enrich American intellectual life—concepts that every educated person intuited as valid descriptions of the reality of contemporary American society.

Even in an area where Hoffman excelled, as in reporting (and mocking) the ingenious and disingenuous propaganda techniques devised and utilized by modern American electronic media, there had already been incisive exposes from as early as the 1950s, i.e., Vance Packard's *The Hidden Persuaders*,[7] which revealed the crass values and sly crafts of Madison Avenue's advertising geniuses and "public relations" genies. And contemporary American political science bulges at its seams with examples of how these technologies and mindgames have been applied to the American electoral system, in selling political candidates much like tampons and bonbons.[8]

All of this, of course, can be used to downgrade Hoffman's originality as an observer of American socio-economic-political phenomena during his days on this globe. After all, no one can deny that little was/is brand new in his delineation of the problem. On the other hand, and we believe this is actually more important, this convergence of Hoffman's views — as a nonprofessional academician, researcher, writer — with those of so many acknowledged experts in the field substantially validates his commentary. He can't be so "off the wall" or "far out" if much of the most respected and influential social analysis of our day, regardless of ideological slant, is in agreement with him.

What is unique to Hoffman's diagnosis of the malaise in America's body politic, is the particular, if not peculiar, way he synthesized it with the wit and turn of phrase that was exclusively his own.

He had his own way of linking a wide variety of symptoms into one syndrome. It was this, along with his distinctive style of presenting it, that was Hoffman's major contribution to the analysis of the illness in contemporary America. Along with the prescription for the remedy, which we will discuss in Part III, the result is the totality of Abbie Hoffman's philosophy for a free and green America.

The Living Fallacy of the Free and Just American Culture

What Abbie Hoffman saw in his lifelong sojourn through the U.S.A., and in his experience as a television personality and viewer, was an America destroying itself in contradiction and hypocrisy. Among its most cherished values were those of rugged individualism and a free and just society. But were these practically consistent? The Pledge of Allegiance to the Flag says: "with liberty and justice for all." But is this possible in praxis? Can there be liberty *and* justice for *all*? Indeed, can there ever be *liberty* for *all*?

Virulent, Unequal Individualism

Hoffman was as much an individual and individualist as anyone. Yet he came to realize that rampant individualism as a cardinal social value was creating a serious problem at the very heart of American society which was, in turn, leading to fundamental problems in the American political system.

What he saw was a cult of individualism fostered in the United States, a deeply entrenched value in self-ism that led most people into personal, social and political isolation and despair. He could not avoid seeing that contemporary America was being overwhelmed by a pseudo-ethic of Number One-ism, much to the detriment of the health and viability of American democracy. He called it "The Lottery Effect"—a conditioned proclivity to "think of ourselves as a nation of self-made winners."[9]

 We think of ourselves as a nation of self-made winners. I call this The Lottery Effect."
Abbie Hoffman

Think of it like this: The world of advertising and sports, both media-centered mega-industries, bombards the American consciousness with slogans like "We're Number One!" and "Winning isn't everything, it's the only thing." As Hoffman noticed, if success is only winning and being number one, very few can be winners. Worse yet, if you're not a winner, then you must be a loser. It's a zero-sum game in America—and the vast majority are doomed to the loser's circle. Sooner or later, this attitude, plus a rigged socio-political mechanism, exacts a heavy psychological toll on most persons in this society, and the situation is getting worse. Or, as Hoffman put it: "The problem is, fewer and fewer number ones can make it."[10]

Being wedded to such a value system means that most people become discouraged and have a heap of trouble maintaining a decent level of self-esteem. What good is it being an individual

> The problem is, fewer and fewer number ones can make it."
>
> *Abbie Hoffman*

if you don't think much of yourself? What is the value of individualism if it creates a society in which the main body of people will eventually be defeated?

This deeply etched notion of competitive individualism was not, in Hoffman's eyes, something that just happened randomly. He came to understand that individualism is a value that is indelibly branded into the American psyche. In fact, it is an integral part of all phases of the American educational process, from the earliest and most obvious forms of it to the continuing educational processes of the mass media—public and commercial.

Conversely, Hoffman was aware of and commented frequently about the paucity of attention paid by American popular education and culture to the offsetting (if not complementary) values of cooperation and community. Consider the Western movie as an American art form. Observe who is lionized: the tough sheriff facing down the outlaws, the masked man in the white hat, the independent rancher rescuing his kidnapped child from marauding savages.

We are told that there is not much drama in the collaborative efforts of farmers or of ordinary citizens and merchants trying to develop small communities. And it is said by those who finance and finagle the megamovie deals that there is no pizazz in the collaborative role of frontier women in razing forests and raising families in the wilderness. Yet such communal efforts manifest an important set of values and travails that helped blaze the American trails and consolidate American civilization on this continent. What is more, these frontier experiences con-

tain many of the same elements of tragedy, suspense, farce and
excitement as any conventional Western movie portrayal of
early frontier life with its chauvinistic idolatry of rugged male
individualism, cow-poking and gun-slinging.

Hoffman was more than alert to the fact that the American
educational system generally elevates and applauds individual
efforts and competitiveness above all else in the classroom. That
clear message is driven home by the rules of the game: home-
work is the product of each individual student (maybe with the
help of the parent); students compete to give the "right" answer;
only one person is selected "valedictorian"; heroes (but rarely
heroines) are those who defy staggering odds and "win."

The way Hoffman saw it: "Education stresses individuality
and personal achievement. Kids rarely learn about collective efforts, or organizing. American heroes are the great loners, the
Ayn Rand egoists . . . A 'career' is for the individual."[11]

 Education stresses individuality and personal
achievement. Kids rarely learn about collective
efforts, or organizing. American heroes are the
great loners, the Ayn Rand egoists . . . A
'career' is for the individual.' "

Abbie Hoffman

The process of indoctrinating the American people into a
contest of long odds continues throughout life and is reinforced
by that relatively small elite that has a relatively large advantage, often from birth. Freedom of opportunity implies a level
playing field, but in real life s/he who is born into cash, stocks,
gold reserves, estates and social privilege has a 95-yard head-
start in the 100-yard dash.

Hoffman's work is liberally sprinkled with references to the
inequality of opportunity for true individualism in America,
and he especially noted that those who have the most of everything make the most of their influence/control of the mass media. He knew that those with economic power transform it into
media clout. These well-placed people firmly believe in win-
lose games because those citizens without material leverage at

the start are sorely handicapped. If the ones with muscle can keep persuading all those in weaker positions to continue playing against them and against each other, then it's "fun, fun, fun 'til daddy takes the T-bird away."

Keep the losers apart by having them vie against one another for the highly improbable goal of becoming a winner and those with the most of what there is to get will probably get more. Responding to this view of reality, Hoffman stated, "The press, the people in power have convinced you that you are separate. You are not . . . . We are all one, with the same hopes and the same fears."[12]

 The press, the people in power have convinced you that you are separate. You are not . . . . We are all one, with the same hopes and the same fears."

Abbie Hoffman

Hoffman's Cooperative, Public Individualism

Here's a major cornerstone to Hoffman's philosophy: we are individuals, true, but we must comprehend and accept the fact that we are interconnected. As was clear throughout his work and life, Hoffman's individuality was constantly linked to personal transcendence, to a greater good, to public-spiritedness, social consciousness and conscientiousness. Hoffman believed that for those people without the personal, material resources of lucre and/or leverage, interpersonal interactions and giving of self were readily available ways to support the growth of personal skills and talents. He saw and wrote with great clarity that the educational system and the various other conduits for those in power downplayed the values of community solidarity and the mutuality of interests of the ordinary working men and women of the United States.

The importance of individual leadership, exalted position or exceptional personal achievements, "celebritydom," was and is highlighted by the present-day system. What is downgraded is the significance and contribution of the unsung heroics of everyday cooperative life and collaborative survival. "There is little encouragement," said Hoffman, "for the idea that workers share a communality of conditions. In fact, relying on the group for strength is pictured as a weakness by the individual."[13]

 There is little encouragement for the idea that workers share a communality of conditions. In fact, relying on the group for strength is pictured as a weakness by the individual."
                                                      Abbie Hoffman

Thus, the American public, by and large, has been successfully brainwashed into a virulent, materialistic egotism. One may think a bit beyond one's self to one's own nuclear or extended family. But that's about as outside-the-self as one will probably get if one buys into the value system procreated by the private and public educational system and by the so-called "independent" mass media networks.

Of course, pockets of resistance to this malignant value system can be found in some individuals and in some churches and universities, but Hoffman saw them being overpowered. He realized that with so much mind-numbing going on, it was exceedingly difficult to stay awake. In fact, many well-intentioned folks just surrender to the steady drumming of me, me, me-ism and stop thinking about any greater good. "We deliberately avoid a global economic vision as well as a social awareness of reality, forcing ourselves to look out for number one."[14]

 We deliberately avoid a global economic vision as well as a social awareness of reality, forcing ourselves to look out for number one."
                                                      Abbie Hoffman

So, if there is any conspiracy here, in the mind of Abbie Hoffman it was an unholy collusion between the losers and the winners to keep on playing the same game with faint to no hope of there being a change in the score: a few big winners and legions of heavy losers. Thus, all are free to play, but, according to Hoffman, if justice is defined as a reasonable or equitable distribution of the material assets of a society among its population, the way the American system is designed and constructed, there is no relationship between such freedom and justice—and that is a major cause of the disease attacking the American polity.

The Inhumanities of Consumerism and Ageism

Another important aspect of this system that produces squads of victors and armies of the vanquished is the definition of winning and losing. Despite protestations of being a God-fearing and spiritual nation, America worships at the shrine of Things and Stuff, adulating worldly possessions and those who accumulate and flaunt the most of them.

Acquiring conspicuous material wealth is the basis of a philosophy of Consumerism that characterizes the foundation of modern American individualism. Citizens are constantly referred to as "consumers"—as though that is a worthy station in life. The more people purchase, the more successful they are seen as being. Poor people don't buy much and losers don't either. But there are so many losers that they are an enormous market anyway. The big winners consume a lot but what they acquire the most of is that which is of greatest value: the best, the rarest, the fastest, the biggest, ad nauseam. In fact, American individualism has come to be defined mostly in terms of what people own and less in terms of what they think, what they dream, how they treat others and what they do. Being individualistic to the young is how they dress, what gadgets they garner (apparel, accessories, autos, computers) and so forth. Sadly, it's the same with the old too.

Abbie Hoffman was hardly the only person to see, describe and dislike this ethos with a passion. He, too, displayed his personal individuality via what he owned, like his shirt composed of an American flag. But he was careful to avoid defining himself by his possessions or material wealth (he gave most of his royalties and speaker's fees to allies and causes and to bail himself out of jail). So, he intentionally gathered very little. He realized that this entire system of consumerism and materialism is based primarily upon the exploitation of the many by the few and, sadly, of the many by the many as well. It isn't only winners who exploit losers. Losers try to exploit as many other losers (the bigger losers) as they can too. This hierarchy of material exploitation that most Americans are part of produces a high level of inhumanity.

In this way, Hoffman was quite anti-capitalist. After all, those with capital (money, equipment, goods, buildings) employ people to use their capital to make products or provide services for a profit. The difference between the cost of the machines, cash, structures and labor and the price of the goods or services produced is a large part of the profit. So, the capitalist (and/or her or his managers) tries to keep the fixed costs down and prices up. The capitalists also try to create artificial demands for their goods and services by playing on the fears and anxieties of the population. Thus, such a system exploits both the laborer and the multitudes of consumers. What bothered Hoffman so much was the exploitation and the many different groups in society that are victimized for the material benefit of so very few — and how they are duped into letting this continue.

In addition to the problem of becoming insulated into self, selfishness and partly into family and labor units, Hoffman foresaw another type of demographic grouping of individuals that was, is and will remain a crucial problem in contemporary America. Back in the 1960s, there was a great fuss made over what was then called "The Generation Gap." The "counterculture" — with its emphasis on social idealism, making love instead of war, distrust of authority, use of psychoactive drugs, plus the accoutrements of longish hair and the costumes of the day — marked a clear delineation between the post-World War II generation and their sons and daughters. The former were much more formal, deferential to authority and materialistic. The latter said they were not, and at least tried to act so at the time. The generational cleavage was characterized by a popular slogan of the day: "Don't trust anyone over thirty." Abbie Hoffman, though not the inventor of the phrase, was an advocate of it.

On the other hand, Hoffman saw this schism as just another division in society that the dominant class utilized for their own ends. On one side was a huge group of young people, flashing their vaunted individuality, revelling in it. On the other side was another large group of Americans who were reaching old age, most of whom dwelled in painful loneliness. They, however, were less enthusiastic about the proceeds their age brought to them. They were alone, true, but suffered in their desolate individualism.

To Abbie Hoffman, both sets of people were being victimized — just like the larger population. Marx had made it easy to understand how the working class was fragmented and in what ways it was kept in a position to be used while usable and trashed when used up.

Hoffman put it this way to the young, of whom he was still one when he said it: "We had been lured into a Madison Avenue trap: the bourgeois romancing of youth. To glorify youth is to hate yourself, because everyone ages."[15]

> We had been lured into a Madison Avenue trap: the bourgeois romancing of youth. To glorify youth is to hate yourself, because everyone ages."
>
> **Abbie Hoffman**

Hoffman understood that, even in opulent America, young people do not have it made. The teenage years, the twenties, are difficult. Most young men and women try desperately to find some kind of personal identity. Decent jobs are not easy to find. One has to learn to "pay dues," start at the bottom, work one's way up. Growing up, trying to find a place in the adult world involves a great deal of psychic stress. One thing young people have, though, which adults do not, is their youth. And it is in both their vulnerabilities and strengths that they can be and are most used to the advantage of those with power and influence who socialize them into accepting hierarchy, consumerism and reinforce their sense that they are different from the older generation.

With the older generation, Hoffman saw another type of exploitation: "When you can be exploited, you are important. When you are old and beyond exploiting, either as a worker or as a consumer, you are no longer important. A functional economic system must be anti-human, as it promotes false values and dooms millions of people to the junkheap."[16]

When you can be exploited, you are important. When you are old and beyond exploiting, either as a worker or as a consumer, you are no longer important. A functional economic system must be anti-human, as it promotes false values and dooms millions of people to the junkheap."

Abbie Hoffman

Hoffman was particularly pained by how people of years are shunted aside in this materialistic, consumer loving society. He saw that most older people are likened to obsolete equipment, something to be deposited out of the way, to be junked. The exceptions, of course, are *well-to-do old people*. He couldn't help but observe the graying of America and how many "senior citizens" are being stowed in decrepit nursing or old-age homes in greater and greater numbers. It is just another symptom of a sick society. "What better example of the inhumanity of the American experience," he wrote, "than the treatment of old people. When you are no longer of any economic use, you are no longer of any human use in America."[17]

What better example of the inhumanity of the American experience than the treatment of old people. When you are no longer of any economic use, you are no longer of any human use in America."

Abbie Hoffman

So, as Hoffman saw it, whether in their youth or old age, the vast majority of Americans are going to fall prey to a system that drains their talent, plays on their individual fears, manipulates their minds and eventually abandons them as useless chattels. United they may stand, so divided they must be kept.

The Continuing Triumphs and Tragedies of Enforced Hypocrisy: Strategy and Tactics

Hoffman was a theorist on the socialization process, on how fundamental cultural values are planted, fertilized and watered. He was particularly interested in the value indoctrination which occurs through the official educational system (schools) and the unofficial educational system (the mass media). Values are like seeds. They don't grow unless they are properly rooted and adequately nurtured. But what struck Hoffman as being particularly sinister and deleterious was that these very same conduits are especially expert at instituting and enforcing a double-standard of ethical, moral and social behavior. Water is good for the orchids, but not good for the daisies.

Obviously, this is not done in a way that is clear to one and all. It probably isn't even administered consciously by many (or any) of those who do it. That's why all political systems are so powerful and effective. There is a subtle, resilient and enduring hypocrisy that undergirds the interconnection between the social, political, and economic systems. This forms a comprehensive structure of incompatible values that works its way into the thoughts and spirit of almost everyone in the country, violating the integrity and independence of all—including its principal beneficiaries. This is the hallmark of American political life, but Hoffman wasn't deceived.

There is, however, another major element that strongly reinforces this cunningly implanted split-value system—a factor that is not gentle to those who fall victim to it. It is the element of force and coercion which is deployed to protect and maintain the pyramids of social, economic and political power and to keep those at the base in their place. It is this combination, physical compulsion intertwined with the double-standard of ethics and morality, what might best be called "*enforced hypocrisy*," that bothered Hoffman deeply.

To Hoffman, this hypocrisy, this two-faced view of reality, permeates America's legal system, its foreign policy, the way the government functions, etc. It makes mockery of much of what is taught about how the system is set up, such as America being a place of "equality of opportunity," where "equal justice under the law" flourishes and where America is "the leader of the free world." Concerning this hypocrisy, Abbie Hoffman wrote, "Until we understand the nature of institutional violence and how it manipulates values and mores to maintain the power of the few, we will forever be imprisoned in the caves of ignorance."[18]

> Until we understand the nature of institutional violence and how it manipulates values and mores to maintain the power of the few, we will forever be imprisoned in the caves of ignorance."
>
> *Abbie Hoffman*

Beyond Orwell and Huxley: The New American Media-Police State

Abbie Hoffman's public, and a good deal of his private, life found him pitted against a phalanx of police agencies and media companies. Being a leading dissident against public policies he found inimical to the health of the commonwealth, plus being a highly visible advocate of conventional and unconventional resistance to the execution of these policies, Hoffman often found himself at the business end of a nightstick or a zoom lens.

If the Bill of Rights was passed to protect those whom government leaders found to be abhorrent and antagonistic, Abbie Hoffman was a champion of that breed. Thus, it is not surprising that he was sensitive to the notion of "police state," the American variant of which he christened "Amerika."

Hoffman saw many manifestations of how this worked against himself during his relatively brief political career. But he also saw it efficiently utilized against many of the downtrodden demographic groupings in American society. From his perspective, depending on which particular laws, regulations and/or policies he opposed at any given time, police actions were utilized to decimate, debilitate if not eliminate, the leadership of these groups or scapegoat them as a way of diverting attention from the real issues and dilemmas confronting life in America.

Much more often than not, the media played along. Although Hoffman and his causes gained greatly from the coverage of his ideas and actions by the American press, he was alert to and disturbed by what he perceived as the greater power of those who pulled the strings in society to maneuver the electronic and print media against him and the causes he espoused.

Even police agencies were adept at shifting the lens of the cameras in a way that spotlighted a false view of reality. For example, Hoffman once noted that "The FBI tries to convince people that dissent is a conspiracy of a few top manipulators rather than a legitimate outpouring of grievances."[19]

 The FBI tries to convince people that dissent is a conspiracy of a few top manipulators rather than a legitimate outpouring of grievances."
Abbie Hoffman

Of course, the FBI was not alone in its use of such gambits. In this regard, Hoffman saw hypocrisy being used as a tactic, in addition to it being basic to the elite's fundamental way of life. It was a new type of coalition, one of the media and the police in an advanced technological society—supposedly devoted to individualism and freedom—that Hoffman detected and blew the whistle on. The subtlety of this hypocrisy made it far more menacing than the more blatant archetypes described in George Orwell's *1984* and Aldous Huxley's *Brave New World*.

It was A.J. Liebling who first thought up the phrase—now conventional wisdom to media critics—"freedom of the press is guaranteed only to those who own one." However, Hoffman was astute enough to realize that owning a printing press, desktop publishing software, or your own camcorder is not the only prerequisite to truly effective freedom of the press in the modern communications age. There is more needed. Much more.

"Repressive tolerance is a real phenomenon. To talk of true

freedom of the press," said Hoffman, "we must talk of the availability of the channels of communication that are designed to
reach the entire population or at least that segment . . . that
might participate in such a dialogue. *Freedom of the press belongs to those who own the distribution system.*"[20] (Hoffman acknowledged that he got this idea from Herbert Marcuse, a well-
known University of California professor at the time).

 Repressive tolerance is a real phenomenon. To
talk of true freedom of the press, we must talk
of the availability of the channels of
communication that are designed to reach the
entire population, or at least that segment of
the population that might participate in such a
dialogue. Freedom of the press belongs to
those who own the distribution system."

Abbie Hoffman

What is more, in a society where the media and government
are not formally part of the same sub-system, the government
not only has to be proficient in learning how to produce public
relations materials (called "propaganda" when done by other
governments), but they have to learn how to sway the media so
that its disinformation will be distributed as "news." This they
accomplish by diverting substantial resources to the task. As we
shall see later, Hoffman's philosophy included many recom-
mendations about how those without such resources could dif-
fuse their own information and opinion by the use of media-
awareness, imagination and craftiness.

Hoffman had some youthful intimacies with this newly-
emerging media-police state through his involvement in the
anti-Vietnam war movement in the mid and late 1960s. But he
saw the more mature version of the media-police state in the
1980s with the so-called "War on Drugs" as its vehicle. He realized that this media-police state tactic was a more serious threat
to the American body politic than what occurred in the 1960s.
Unlike the 1960s when the malignancy only attacked marginal
parts (mostly the counterculture and Black rebels), in the 1980s

the media-police state was metastasizing in a vital organ (the workforce) and becoming more lethal as it grew.

The American Drug-Industrial Complex

Back in the sixties, when American armed forces were bogged down in the boondocks of Vietnam, the few in power were being outflanked by a ragtag group of young radicals, university intellectuals and a newly enlightened group of media pros. These people, through new methods of organization, protest and alternative media, were getting their message through to large segments of the public, that is: those running the military-industrial complex, in league with those in government, were lying to the American people about the true nature, costs and outcomes of the Vietnam War.

As the tide of public opinion slowly turned, those in power resorted increasingly to illicit activities to maintain control. Among these were military surveillance of the American protest movement, extensive undercover infiltration of legitimate political organizations by police agencies, trumped up charges that led to many arrests and trials (including Hoffman's), etc. In other words, the military-industrial complex was using police state tactics to defeat the counterculture's anti-war movement. It was an offensive of gross illegitimacy by those in power against those who were legally trying to oust them from power.

Although this powerful elite lost that battle on the home-front—many of them losing elections, resigning in disgrace from office, and some of them going to jail for various acts of government lawlessness—they did not forget what happened, nor did their allies and successors to power. Hoffman was well aware that the struggle for and against totalitarianism on American soil has been and will be forever.

Its present-day incarnation was born in the early years of the presidency of Ronald Reagan. That it occurred during a period of Republican ascendancy fits well within a pattern of twentieth century American political life. Various and sundry police state methods flourished against the labor union movement during the eras of McKinley and Theodore Roosevelt; against the alcohol habit of many American citizens during the presidencies of Harding, Coolidge and Hoover; against alleged internal subversion during the Eisenhower years (spearheaded by Republican Senator Joseph McCarthy); against the New Left and Black Power movements in the Nixon years; and against drugs favored by dissident and minority groups during the Reagan and Bush reign.

In all these situations, there were hidden agendas, to wit: a desire to maintain hegemony over the American workforce (to take as much and give as little as possible) and a desire to tell other people how to live their private lives and to use force to do so. Hoffman saw covert reasons behind the rhetorical goal of achieving what is obviously an impossible mission: a "drug-free America." Clearly this can only be done by effectively outlawing and eliminating the consumption of all beer, liquor and tobacco products — a goal as realistic as criminalizing the act of breathing.

The real goal, in his view, is to dominate the segments of the American population who are the major victims of the move from an industrial-based economy to a high-tech and service economy, i.e., the working class and ethnic minorities. The goal is to maintain discipline over those elements of society who will be hit hardest by the transfer of American industrial jobs to third world countries (where labor unions are either weak or nonexistent and where local police states do not have to contend with the U.S. Constitution and the Bill of Rights).

 Drugs are being scapegoated in an attempt to avoid making badly needed social and economic changes in a disintegrating society."
Abbie Hoffman

Thus, a new kind of domestic alliance has evolved, one between the most conservative or reactionary elements of the ruling elite, many government leaders and officials, a myriad of police agencies, the mass media and a wide array of professionals whose expertise involves certain specified psychoactive drugs. This coalition's purpose is severalfold.

First, as Hoffman pointed out many times, this league is pushing a moral agenda through government as a way of maximizing social control while at the same time using it as a "red herring" to distract attention from what is really going on. In Hoffman's words, "Drugs are being scapegoated in an attempt to avoid making badly needed social and economic changes in a disintegrating society."[21]

Or, as he stated it elsewhere, "Urine testing on Wall Street, Main Street or Mill Street is a distraction meant to take our mind off a crumbling economy, a shrinking workforce, and a citizenry being cowered into giving up its rights along with its urine."[22]

 Urine testing on Wall Street, Main Street or Mill Street is a distraction meant to take our mind off a crumbling economy, a shrinking workforce, and a citizenry being cowered into giving up its rights along with its urine."

Abbie Hoffman

Even worse, from Hoffman's perspective, is that this new media-police state is determined to break the spirit of the populace. Drug tests have the extra dash of humiliation that make the

 I suspect that the real appeal of the urine test lies in its control over a workforce that had become dangerously suspicious and potentially powerful. Pulling workers' pants down lets 'em know who's boss. It threatens their jobs and dignity."

Abbie Hoffman

control complete. "I suspect that the real appeal of the urine test lies in its control over the workforce that had become dangerously suspicious and potentially powerful. Pulling workers' pants down lets 'em know who's boss. It threatens their jobs and dignity."[23]

None of this could occur, though, without the active partnership of the so-called independent and free press, particularly that part of it that has the means to reach into the vast majority of American living rooms. During the early stages of the Vietnam War, the press served as a cheerleader for and a misinformation outlet of those who declared and waged the war. It also dismissed (as "conspiracy theory") complaints about the internal and illegal war being waged by the government on the homefront against those who protested and worked against that war.

It was not until the Tet Offensive in the late 1960s, during which the true strength of the Vietcong become obvious—much to the embarrassment of America's governmental, military and media elite—that the press began to show a glimmer of its vaunted independence. Once that happened, it was the beginning of the end to the major enforced hypocrisy of the day.

Most of the time, or at least in the early stages of external or internal oppression, the media works hand-in-glove with the state and industrial apparatuses that have the most to gain from them. Hoffman was extremely cynical about the degree to which America's mass media is truly free to investigate, criticize and publicize any alternative views to the official viewpoint. "If you believe America has a free press, it just means you haven't thought about it enough."[24]

 If you believe America has a free press, it just means you haven't thought about it enough."
Abbie Hoffman

Ravaging Mother Earth

One of the most important shifts in latter day American politics has been a new ecological awareness that has spawned a whole new global movement. This movement was conceived in the 1960s, born on Earth Day 1970, enjoyed a robust adolescence in the 1980s and promises young adulthood in the 1990s.

Although Hoffman was not formally associated with environmentalism, as a major leader of the sixties counterculture—which included many of the pioneer environmentalists of the day—he was in fact more closely involved than most people realized. The counterculture was a mix of new values that sprouted a distinctive "lifestyle," one characterized by such features as: a much more liberal attitude towards sex and psychedelic drugs, a desire for more democratic ways to run "the system," a commitment to equality among the sexes, a greater concern for a cleaner and sounder environment, to name a few. Those in the counterculture favored all these things (more or less) and tried to support organizations that favored any of them.

It is not out of character, then, or a stretch of his political beliefs, that Abbie Hoffman surfaced, after years of being a fugitive from the police in the 1970s, as a leader of an environmental action group in upstate New York. Early in his "career," he helped organize a "media event" against Con Edison (the New York utility company) to publicize its role in poisoning the air: "Our guerrilla band attacked . . . on cue, soot bombs exploded in offices, smudge pots billowed thick smoke in lobbies, black crepe paper encircled the building, and a huge banner hung across the front door: BREATHING IS BAD FOR YOUR HEALTH."[25]

> Our guerrilla band attacked . . . on cue, soot bombs exploded in offices, smudge pots billowed thick smoke in lobbies, black crepe paper encircled the building, and a huge banner hung across the front door:
> **BREATHING IS BAD FOR YOUR HEALTH."**
> *Abbie Hoffman*

Proving this one example of Hoffman's environmental activism was no fluke, he was working on another environmental protection issue in eastern Pennsylvania at the time of his death.

Hoffman was not a flaming environmentalist anymore than he was a fanatic libertarian. When he was living "underground" in the St. Lawrence River area, he came to understand that framing the problem simply in terms of "jobs versus the environment" was bogus. First, it was oversimplified. Second, it stacked the odds in favor of one economic factor in the equation: a short-sighted one.

The real issues were complex and long-range. For one thing, governmental interference with the natural order sometimes created greater economic hardship over time than existed before. The development of the St. Lawrence Seaway in the 1950s was a prime example of that.

According to Hoffman, (a) instead of the Seaway producing an economic boom in that locale, more and more people found themselves with a lot of unpaid leisure time; (b) instead of profits, the Seaway ran in the red and the American taxpayers had to foot the bill; (c) the project was a major factor in bankrupting the railroad industry in that part of the country.

But these were only the most direct, obviously negative impacts on the economy. What was more difficult to ascertain were the indirect, long-range calamities for the entire ecology of the region which supported the unique economic foundation of the local culture. In other words, a new economic order would be forged out of a devastated environment, one that would mainly benefit powerful, well-organized outside interests at the expense of the disorganized, relatively docile local workers, farmers, merchants, etc.

Although the St. Lawrence Seaway had already perpetrated great financial havoc on many who lived along its banks, a new scheme was hatched shortly after Hoffman's arrival thereabouts. The U.S. Army Corps of Engineers, which lusted for a new, grand scale construction, had masterminded a new blueprint to gouge a year-round, ice-free pathway through the oft-frozen Seaway. They reasoned that this would finally make the initial venture profitable and it would demonstrate the feasibility of "winter navigation," long a pet vision of the Corps.

Hoffman, in his new role as organizer for an environmental organization called "Save The River," researched the issue and concluded that the plan would be an environmental disaster — to the river, the wetlands, the wildlife, the shoreline and, of course, the river people themselves. If anyone was going to get "jobs" out of this, it wouldn't be the St. Lawrence river rats, it would be the Army Corps of Engineers, its cronies and its political patrons.

This new ploy squared with Hoffman's overall philosophy about how certain people exploited others economically through the machinations of big government. In this case, though, the exploitation wasn't through police and/or military action or agencies. Rather, it was through what many see as a relatively useful government agency, one that builds important projects that are good for America and that bring great pride and credit to the nation.

No one can deny that the U.S. Army Corps of Engineers has accomplished a great deal for the country, but like the military and police, it has a significant darkside, one that sullies its image and reputation. Hoffman described the Corps like this: "They are unquestionably the most gung-ho, can-do organization in the entire federal bureaucracy. If the money was there, the Corps would move mountains from Colorado to Iowa. Theirs is not to reason why, theirs is to submit the bill and try . . . . The Corps moves like a Supreme Being. It doesn't build, it creates. Its 45,000 public relations experts, lawyers, and contractors directed by a few hundred army brass at the top are almost unbeatable in the field. Almost."[26]

 They are unquestionably the most gung-ho, can-do organization in the entire federal bureaucracy. If the money was there, the Corps would move mountains from Colorado to Iowa. Theirs is not to reason why, theirs is to submit the bill and try . . . . The Corps moves like a Supreme Being. It doesn't build, it creates. Its 45,000 public relations experts, lawyers, and contractors directed by a few hundred Army brass at the top are almost unbeatable in the field. Almost."

Abbie Hoffman

Instead of being the Master Builders, the Army Corps of Engineers was a destructive force, a *very* destructive one, not only to the local economy and local culture, but to the natural harmony of the regional environment and beyond. The Corps was also a subset of a complicated system of despoliation, exploitation and power manipulation that was at the heart of so many of the other problems Hoffman dealt with throughout his lifetime.

Summary

Being true to great traditions in American political satire and political philosophy, Abbie Hoffman's view of the polity (in this case the United States of America during the final third of the twentieth century) is not a pretty picture. He saw the body politic as a power system that has long been supported by a complex, sophisticated and two-faced value system, one that is aided and abetted in its control by an adroit, vicious and avaricious elite. The educational system and mass media, financially supported and managed by elements of the elite, germinate and nurture these values so that almost everyone within American society believes in them, despite the fact that they are replete with systematic and systemic inconsistency and contradiction.

According to Hoffman, to minimize the discrepancies, the educational and media centers overplay those values that foster control by the elite and induce separation of the many, and downplay, insult or ignore those that might unite the multitudes. In addition, physical compulsion and/or intimidation are used tactically to strengthen the disuniting values and diminish the collaborative ones.

When opposition reaches a level that interferes with policies mostly beneficial to this elite, an increasingly intrusive public and private intelligence and police network comes into play at all levels of politics and work. In interaction with the media and educational systems, these centers of power are adept at deflecting attention from real problems and issues and focusing, instead, upon other issues (like the need for more and better weapons systems or "just saying no" to disfavored drugs) that help pave the way for greater internal surveillance and domestic spread of police powers.

These interactions are part of a traditional tendency in American politics. But they are also part of a modern type of police statism geared to obliterate dissent and deter the labor force from reacting against policies intended to decrease its share of the national wealth.

What this adds up to in Hoffman's philosophy is a new industrial police state under the trappings of individualism and freedom. It is artfully styled to increase the material interests of the small controlling elite at the expense of the ordinary citizens' share of material comfort, health, personal freedom and security.

This new industrial police state has also arisen at the expense of the sustainability of the environment of the American nation — from twelve-mile limit to twelve-mile limit — including the earth below and the air above. Those who gain from exploitation of the environment are not married to the American environment they rape since their ill-gotten gains provide them with domiciles and recreation spots in relatively unspoiled havens and harbors around the world, or they do not reside in the particular sites they drain or damage for their own profits. They are, in some sense, betrayers of their land and its people.

In the mind's eye of Abbie Hoffman, the future of America, left to the devices of those who currently control its centralized sources of power and influence, is sad to behold. It is a future of increasing social injustice, official suppression and ecological devastation and desecration . . . unless, of course, the American people themselves do something about it as soon as possible.

Being true to the timeless profession of philosopher, Hoffman had a lot to say about how to spur the public to action. He spoke fervently about how each and every citizen who agrees (at least in part) with his assessment of the present, and the imminent possibility of the future he described, can act today, tomorrow and forever to help make the future of America as *free and green as it can be.*

Part Three

Standing on the Shoulders of Giants:
Hoffman in an American Philosophical Context

I t should be pretty obvious that by detailing the flaws in a political system, philosophers cannot help but display their
own value systems, as well as the short- and long-term futures
they prefer. There are several values and preferences fundamental to classic American political thought inherent in Abbie Hoffman's political writing, satire and organizing.

In this Part III, we will show how Hoffman is a late twentieth
century bearer of the philosophical torch lit, carried and relayed
by such illustrious predecessors as Thomas Jefferson, Henry
David Thoreau, Ralph Waldo Emerson and John Dewey. This
intellectual continuity includes such ideas as: (1) the challenge
of strengthening and expanding American democracy; (2) the
necessity of perpetuating the spirit of the American revolution;
(3) the honor and costs to an individual for speaking the truth
and acting against unrepresentative, excessive and/or arbitrary
authority.

We noted earlier that much of what Hoffman thought and
wrote was well within the conventional boundaries of American political philosophy. But renewal of these ideas in light of
new conditions is an important job. It is also noteworthy that
these ageless themes are couched by Hoffman in modern parlance with a contemporary spin. Hoffman, in his vibrant and
earthy prose and tone, parades these ideas and ideals before the

eyes of those willing to see anew, before all who wish to inherit a bold and eternal American political tradition.

Hoffman is subject to the epithet of "popularizer." He would be the first to laugh it off. The glaring irony is that a pro-democratic political philosophy that the average person finds hard to read and understand is a contradiction in terms. Hoffman's version of American democratic thought welcomes one and all. It is entertaining, provocative and fiery.

All this is not meant to say that Hoffman's political thinking is simply refurbished clothes in a thrift shop. His brand of political satire was, actually, a series of experiments in the politics of modern media. His books bristle with concepts, theories and analyses of how television, radio and newspapers can be used as channels by which to: 1) demonstrate alternative political realities; 2) educate the public on creative, engaging forms of political action and reaction; and 3) help mobilize and redirect public opinion. All of these are signature contributions by Hoffman to the ever growing encyclopedia of American political philosophy—details of which will occupy a later section of this part of the book.

Democracy, Individualism and the Continuing Process of Political Change

When we say that Abbie Hoffman's main political values were democracy, enlightened individualism and the continuing process of political change, we are also saying that this was his image of a better world. In addition, Hoffman understood that democracy, enlightened individualism and the continuing process of political change were also the *ways* to a better world. The means and the ends are one and the same. This is not as contradictory as it may seem. ·

Hoffman spent a lot of his time thinking, writing, planning, and rehearsing. He realized that a philosophy with concepts like democracy, individualism and continuing political change was not and could not be a mere abstraction. These words refer to *living processes*, not static states. They are innately dynamic. So he thought about them, acted them out, and reflected on them as the central tenets of his own action philosophy—just like those in whose footsteps he followed.

More Democracy: Jefferson and Dewey

The first great political philosophical debate in the United States of America, in the immediate aftermath of its agonizing birth by blood and flames, was about how much democracy is healthy to any political body. The period between the British surrender at Yorktown to George Washington in 1781 and the ratification of the Bill of Rights in 1791 witnessed a ferocious battle of conflicting beliefs. On one side were those who preached the virtues of individual liberty, limited government and direct democracy. On the other side were those who yearned for a large, strongly centralized government controlled by men with wealth (and, presumably, wisdom and vision). During the Constitutional ratification period, the latter called themselves the "Federalists" and those who fought them doggedly acquired the unfortunately negative label of "Anti-federalists."

In truth, though, the Anti-federalists were (in the main) pro-democrats. In fact, if it had not been for their heroic stand, there never would have been a Bill of Rights woven into the fabric of the U.S. Constitution. Foremost among them was Thomas Jefferson: revolutionary, architect, statesman, president of the United States, educator—and political philosopher *extraordinaire*.

Jefferson, the mastermind behind and sparkplug of the Declaration of Independence, was and remains one of the most prominent democratic theorists and philosophers in the history of humankind. He distrusted the rich, vainglorious American aristocracy almost as much as he despised the British nobles whom he helped banish from American soil. It was his view that the upper class was a pack of "wolves" who preyed upon hard-working ordinary farmers, laborers, and craftsman—whom he likened to "sheep."

Mr. Jefferson, the Anti-federalist's Anti-federalist, knew that the plutocrats (those who believe in rule-by-the-rich) coveted ever more money and control and that a strong and centralized government—despite the fancy rhetoric of the Federalists to the contrary—would become an engine for their greed so that they could more systematically milk and bilk the populace. His solution was sharp and pointed: keep government to a minimum; keep it pale and puny so the wolves wouldn't be able to use it to slaughter too many lambs. Government's primary role is to keep the domestic peace, with little else to do except keep its hands out of the population's pockets. Or, as Jefferson himself said in his first inaugural address: "Still one thing more—fellow citizens—a wise and frugal government, which shall restrain men from injuring one another, shall leave them otherwise free to regulate their own pursuits of industry and improvement, and shall not take from the mouth of labor the bread it has earned. This is the sum of good government . . . ." [1]

> Still one thing more—fellow citizens—a wise and frugal government, which shall restrain men from injuring one another, shall have them otherwise free to regulate their own pursuits of industry and improvement, and shall not take from the mouth of labor the bread it has earned. This is the sum of good government . . . ."
>
> *Thomas Jefferson*

This should not be read as evidence that the man who became America's third president was a raving anarchist or flaming libertarian. He believed in government. But he believed in a government in which the supreme power remained in the hands of the average citizen. Such power was only effective,

> . . . were it left to me to decide whether we should have a government without newspapers or newspapers without a government, I should not hesitate a moment to prefer the latter."
>
> *Thomas Jefferson*

though, when the entire citizenry had sufficient information upon which to base informed and reasoned judgments about the important matters of the time. That is why, in Jefferson's opinion, " . . . were it left to me to decide whether we should have a government without newspapers or newspapers without a government, I should not hesitate a moment to prefer the latter."[2]

So, the quintessence of democracy, in the fertile mind of Jefferson, was that the real power to decide should reside in the educated, collective judgment of the American people. Elitists of his day, as well as of any day, argued that the average person did not have a good enough background, enough data, or the burning desire to make the kind of complex judgments on crucial social, economic and political topics that only the well-to-do could, should and would make. Despite this prejudice, Jefferson did not budge from his fervent belief in the righteous exercise of political power by the public. "I know no safe depository of the ultimate powers of the society but the people themselves; and if we think them not enlightened enough to exercise their control with a wholesome discretion, the remedy is not to take it from them, but to inform their discretion by education."[3]

 I know no safe depository of the ultimate powers of the society but the people themselves; and if we think them not enlightened enough to exercise their control with a wholesome discretion, the remedy is not to take it from them, but to inform their discretion by education."

Thomas Jefferson

Thus, Jefferson saw a lifeline between "strong democracy" and sufficient information to and proper education of the masses. This faith in the enlightened common person as the bulwark of American democracy has persisted over time, despite its many detractors and a well stocked arsenal of verbal ammunition launched against it by well-placed American oligarchists. Its most recent deep defense was constructed by John Dewey, whose philosophy of popular education fit well with Jefferson's notions of improving politics by broadening, nurturing and honing the minds of the people themselves.

Dewey understood full well that democracy was not merely a form of government. He recognized that American democracy was much less than advertised because despite the flowery tributes to the American democratic way of life, undemocratic — if not downright anti-democratic — ways of thought and behavior were drilled into the nation's youth in numerous venues. "In homes and in schools, the places where the essentials of character are supposed to be formed, the usual procedure is settlement of issues, intellectual and moral, by appeal to the 'authority' of parent, teacher, or textbook. Dispositions formed under such conditions are so inconsistent with the democratic method that in a crisis they may be aroused to act in positively anti-democratic ways for anti-democratic ends."[4]

 In homes and in schools, the places where the essentials of character are supposed to be found, the usual procedure is settlement of issues, intellectual and moral, by appeal to the 'authority' of parent, teacher, or textbook. Dispositions formed under such conditions are so inconsistent with the democratic method that in a crisis they may be aroused to act in positively anti-Democratic ways for anti-Democratic ends."

John Dewey

Dewey may have had an inkling of the future growth of the American military-industrial complex and its highly sophisticated public relations (propaganda) mills that equate good citizenship with lockstep support of authority and authoritative decision-making. Back in 1929, he observed that "the most militaristic of nations secures the loyalty of its subjects not by physical force but through the power of ideas and emotions. It cultivates ideals of loyalty, of solidarity, and common devotion to a common cause."[5]

Thus, it was logical for Dewey to conclude that a counter-education had to be devised and set in motion. The aim was to counteract anti-democratic conditioning and to socialize young

Americans so that they could begin to achieve their self-potential as independent-minded citizens. Self-respect and individual growth are two key preconditions for assuming the

 The most militaristic of nations secures the loyalty of its subjects not by physical force but through the power of ideas and emotions. It cultivates ideals of loyalty, of solidarity, and common devotion to a common cause."
John Dewey

responsibilities, privileges and duties of citizenship in any true democracy.

Dewey believed this was possible, even in an advanced militaristic or paramilitary society. He was certain that despite the use of brute force, pervasive social engineering, and/or diabolically clever media and educational manipulations—the damage to the psyche was reversible. In his words: " . . . our uniformity of thought is much more superficial than it seems to be. . . . It goes far enough to effect suppression of original quality of thought, but not far enough to achieve enduring unity. Its superficial character is evident in its instability. All agreement of thought obtained by external means, by repression and intimidation, however subtle, and by calculated propaganda and publicity, is of necessity superficial."[6]

 All agreement of thought obtained by external means, by repression and intimidation, however subtle, and by calculated propaganda and publicity, is of necessity superficial."
John Dewey

Dewey put most of his eggs into the education basket. His cardinal contribution to the maintenance and growth of democracy in America has been through his philosophical analysis of it and his offerings on how to develop "democratic education" grounded in a "democratic theory of education."[7]

More Democracy: Hoffman

Abbie Hoffman will not go down in the annals of American democratic thought in the same rank as Jefferson or Dewey. In the context of his own philosophy, however, Hoffman, like many before (and after) him, grasped the importance of the adage that the best medicine for a diseased democracy is a brimming tablespoon of more potent democracy.

Like Jefferson, he respected the native abilities of the ordinary working person and the collective judgment of the people. Like Jefferson, he bubbled over with suspicion of the wolves. Like Dewey, he understood that the need for more democracy transcends government and that every key institution of American society, including our educational system, economic system, and media, is woefully deficient in democratic values and practices. What he added to these philosophers' thinking were applications of their and his pro-democratic faith in order to help deal with twentieth-century American conundrums.

One of the major sources of Hoffman's democratic ideas and values is found in a flyer designed, written and distributed by him during the 1968 Democratic National Convention in Chicago. Titled "Revolution Towards a Free Society," it contained a potpourri of pro-democratic sentiments and the beginning of an integrated democratic plan for the future.

 We demand . . . a society based on humanitarian cooperation and equality, a society which allows and promotes the creativity present in all people and especially our youth."

Abbie Hoffman

Echoing Jefferson and Dewey, in the flyer "A Yippie" (one of Hoffman's countless *noms de plumes*) lists a series of "demands" as part of the platform of the so-called "Youth International Party" (known as "Yippie"). "We demand . . . a society based on humanitarian cooperation and equality, a society which allows and promotes the creativity present in all people and especially our youth."[8]

In relation to the American educational system, Hoffman emulated Dewey by thrusting students into the forefront of curriculum development by making them personally responsible for their own program of learning. He was also an early proponent of strong, hands-on community involvement in public education. Moreover, as an outgrowth of the general movement for widespread citizen participation in all aspects of society, Hoffman wanted students to play a role in virtually every phase of educational decision-making. Thus, the Yippie program issued the challenge: "Be realistic, demand the impossible: a restructured educational system which provides the student power to determine his course of study and allows for student participation in over-all policy planning. Also an educational system which breaks down its barriers between school and community. A system which uses the surrounding community as a classroom so that students learn directly the problems of the people."[9]

 Be realistic, demand the impossible: a restructured educational system which provides the student power to determine his course of study and allows for student participation in over-all policy planning. Also an educational system which breaks down its barriers between school and community. A system which uses the surrounding community as a classroom so that students learn directly the problems of the people."

Abbie Hoffman

Hoffman was not oblivious, though, to the need for more and better democracy in the political system itself. During the heightened intensity of student demonstrations on many campuses and street demonstrations against the Vietnam War, he kept his eyes trained on the bigger picture—what a more representative system of government might look like.

Once again, Hoffman's ideas were at the leading edge of what has come to be a movement towards more direct democracy in the United States through the use of electronic media. Since the early 1970s, certain futurists, political scientists and democratic technologists have been experimenting with a wide variety of processes that might best be called "teledemocracy" or "electronic democracy."[10] Hoffman, like a few others including Erich Fromm,[11] saw a need for this even earlier. Again, we find his clarion call for this kind of futuristic democracy in the Yippie Program of 1968: "Be realistic, demand the impossible: A political system which is more streamlined and responsive to the needs of all the people regardless of age, sex or race. Perhaps a national referendum system conducted via television or a telephone voting system."[12]

 Be realistic, demand the impossible: A political system which is more streamlined and responsive to the needs of all the people regardless of age, sex or race. Perhaps a national referendum system conducted via television or a telephone voting system."
Abbie Hoffman

Another area ripe for democratization which was of major interest to Hoffman was that of economic and industrial production. In this regard, Hoffman was far from being in the *avant garde*. Nonetheless, he saw the importance of combining a general democratic front in education and politics with that of economic democracy.

His notion of economic democracy was much along the lines of that which had been successfully tested in the American workplace and had been effectively adopted in Sweden and Denmark. His notions about how to democratize both large and small manufacturing were quite similar to the method by which one country became the most efficient and fearsome industrial power of our time, i.e., Japan.

Hoffman understood that the key to economic democracy was to involve the creative powers and the natural intelligence of the worker in all functions of the production process — the epitome of workplace democratization. He also seemed to envision an alternative economics, one coming into prominence in the 1990s, one that would make private corporations responsible to the many environments upon which they locate their operations and draw their profits. This includes the local communities and the natural environments from which they extract their natural resources and strew their wastes. Hoffman saw economic democracy as being defined by stretching the range of workers' responsibilities for their products and multiplying the debts of the manufacturing companies to compensate for the degradation of their environs. Hoffman offered two solutions to the workplace crisis. The first is "the worker participation model used in Scandinavia. There employees are made *wholly* accountable for a manufacturing process from start to finish . . . . The second insists that business must be made more responsible to the community than it is now. . . . This is called economic democracy."[13]

> Two solutions to the workplace crisis — "The worker participation model used in Scandinavia. There employees are made *wholly* responsible for a manufacturing process from start to finish . . . . The second insists that business must be made more accountable to the community than it is now. . . . This is called economic democracy."
>
> **Abbie Hoffman**

The importance Hoffman attributed to democracy in his political philosophy also penetrated into the way he directed and acted out his ideas for "revolutionary" changes in American society. As a media-created "leader" of the counterculture, Hoffman scoffed at the American notion of leadership. At one point, during the 1968 political upheaval in Chicago, he affirmed his view that "There are no spokesmen for the Yippies . . . . We are all our own leaders."[14]

Throughout his writings, one detects a benign obedience to the greater glory of "*participatory democracy*" in all phases of the unfolding historical process of which he claims Hoffman

 There are no spokesmen for the yippies . . . .
We are all our own leaders."
                                         Abbie Hoffman

was but a bit player. As a true-blue democrat, he sermonized on the all-important contribution of each soldier in the pro-democratic mission.

There should be no hierarchy in the value of anyone's contribution to the mission—whether that contribution was in hatching plans, organizing, painting signs or faces, being hauled off to a barbed-wire holding pen, meditating, haranguing, xeroxing pamphlets, or even making love, not war. He wanted a "high degree of involvement" from everyone committed to the cause of more democracy in America. "The people

 The people winning these battles don't sit
around complaining about apathy; instead,
they are actively 'doing democracy.' That's
right—doing democracy. Democracy is more
than a place you live in, more than a belief.
Democracy is a skill, something you learn and
do. You don't do it, you don't have it."
                                         Abbie Hoffman

winning these battles don't sit around complaining about apathy; instead, they are actively 'doing democracy.' That's right— doing democracy. Democracy is more than a place you live in, more than a belief. Democracy is a skill, something you learn and do. You don't do it, you don't have it."[15]

Acting his philosophy out, "doing democracy," also helped convey the image (without having to pay for advertisements on network television) of a titillating day-glo politics in vivid contrast to the humdrum, battleship-gray politics of "The System."

Again expressing his opinion on how important respect for each citizen is to the success of democratic change in America, Hoffman stated: "A populist movement must allow people to define their own space, their own motives, to be their own critics."[16]

 A Populist movement must allow people to define their own space, their own motives, to be their own critics."

Abbie Hoffman

If a movement didn't live up to this practice, it was democratic/populist in name only and the result would be politics-as-usual. But, if a movement truly tapped into the vast reservoir of ideas and talent and valiantly hung in there, then and only then the dream of democracy would become realized: "Democracy means having the courage and persistence to make the dream of a free people come true."[17]

 Democracy means having the courage and persistence to make the dream of a free people come true."

Abbie Hoffman

The Continuing American Revolution and True Patriotic Individualism

Historians are prone to putting a fence of time around political revolutions — even though they are not so quick to do so for economic ones (the Industrial Revolution) or social ones (the feminist movement). Thus, history texts say that the American Revolution started in 1776 and ended in Yorktown in 1781; the French Revolution started in 1789 and ended in 1793; the Russian Revolution started and ended in 1917. That kind of idea dominates history classes in most educational systems.

In the real world, though, political rebellions and revolutions are never-ending processes, just like economic and social revolutions. One need only live in the American South in the 1990s to appreciate the fact that the Civil War did not end in the

 I hold it, that a little rebellion, now and then, is a good thing, and as necessary in the political world as storms in the physical."

Thomas Jefferson

1860s and that its formal (and textbook) "ending" only began a perennial process of social, economic and political ebbs and flows in that great American region.

Thomas Jefferson knew the ongoing nature of political change well and—being a dedicated revolutionary—embraced it lovingly: "I hold it, that a little rebellion, now and then, is a good thing, and as necessary in the political world as storms in the physical."[18]

He also believed that sometimes a situation could occur when a government's actions and policies became so threatening to the continued liberty of the citizenry (the wolves became

 What country before ever exisited a century and half without a rebellion . . . . The tree of liberty must be refreshed from time to time with the blood of patriots and tyrants. It is its natural manure."

Thomas Jefferson

too voracious), that at least some bloodshed was inevitable in order to restore the required amount of freedom. In fact, Jefferson was certain that such moments of hard truth were destined to happen at least occasionally. "What country before ever existed a century and half without a rebellion . . . . The tree of liberty must be refreshed from time to time with the blood of patriots and tyrants. It is its natural manure."[19]

John Dewey also feared the negative impact of characterizing the words and works of dead revolutionaries as gospel truths that must be idolized and revered. To do so would be to create stagnant traditions that would by their very nature become wellsprings of discontent and tyranny. The American revolution was a triumph of *individual liberty*. But liberty cannot only be defined and enshrined in terms of a particular political victory at a particular time against a particular order. It must be won time and time again against any imposed order. As Dewey saw it: "Traditional ideas are more than irrelevant. They are an encumbrance; they are the chief obstacle to the formation of a new individuality integrated within itself and with a liberated function in the society wherein it exists."[20]

 Traditional ideas are more than irrelevant. They are an encumbrance; they are the chief obstacle to the formation of a new individuality . . . ."

John Dewey

A *new individuality*. The spirit of the American Revolution, then, is a renewal of individuality in the face of what is perceived as any emerging order that oppresses the spirit of American freedom. This is the continuing spirit of the American Revolution, and it is not limited to what is artificially narrowed to "political" and "governmental" life. It extends to all aspects of social interaction.

According to Dewey: "Political apathy such as has marked our thought for many years past is due fundamentally to mental confusion arising from lack of consciousness of any vital connection between politics and daily affairs."[21]

Dewey's emphasis on the Continuing American Revolution for individual freedom in *all* corners of American life resonates with the thinking of two earlier American philosophical giants upon whose shoulders Hoffman also stands—Ralph Waldo Emerson and Henry David Thoreau.

In his day, Ralph Waldo Emerson was an avid apostle and ardent advocate of the Continuing American Revolution. His objective was to recruit true individualists in the war against what he, in his own conscience, believed to be the principal

 Political apathy such as has marked our thought for many years past is due fundamentally to mental confusion arising from lack of consciousness of any vital connection between politics and daily affairs."

John Dewey

forms of American oppression of the hour. Merle Curti, one of America's leading chroniclers of American intellectual history, observes:

> Emerson expressed a central tenet of reform philosophy which inspired men and women in their efforts to re-form dress and diet in the interest of universal health, to uproot capital punishment and imprisonment for debt, slavery, intemperance, war and prostitution, and to agitate for the full rights of women, the humane treatment of the insane and the criminal, and even the overthrow of such venerable institutions as the family, private property and the state itself. . . . *[Emerson] put his finger on the essential faith of the reformer when he assumed that institutions exist to be improved, that man can improve them along with himself, that the law of human society, like that of physical nature, is one of change.*"[22]

Or, from the pen of Emerson himself—forgiving him the sexist language of his epoch—"What is a man born for but to be a reformer, a re-maker of what man has made; a renouncer of lies; a restorer of truth and good, imitating that great Nature which embosoms us all, and which sleeps no moment on an old past, but every hour repairs herself, yielding us every morning a new day, and with every pulsation a new life?"[23]

Emerson's good friend Henry David Thoreau was equally up to the task of exalting American individual liberty in opposition to renewed governmental and social oppression—in all its

Machiavellian machinations. Thoreau was committed to a "private war against the herd-spirit, against materialism and conformity, against smugness and hypocrisy, against injustice and slavery."[24]

Thoreau's opinion of the state was also neither sanguine nor benign, to say the least. According to Curti, "Thoreau developed

 What is a man born for but to be a reformer, a remaker of what man has made; a renouncer of lies; a restorer of truth and good, imitating that great nature which embosoms us all, and which sleeps no moment on an old past, but every hour repairs herself, yielding us every morning a new day, and with every pulsation a new life?"

Ralph Waldo Emerson

the thesis that the state is potentially or actually an evil institution inimical to the freedom of the individual."[25] In any case in which an American citizen felt that the state was acting against her or his "sense of right," it became the duty of the citizen to resist, to engage in an act of "civil disobedience." Of course, this could, and probably would, lead to serious repercussions for the citizen expressing her or his moral indignation. These would include loss of material wealth or convenience and perhaps a temporary loss of physical freedom, e.g., imprisonment.

 Most of the luxuries and many of the so-called comforts of life are not only dispensable, but positive hindrances to the elevation of mankind."

Henry David Thoreau

To Thoreau, such a loss of liberty was of lesser importance than the spiritual gains: "Most of the luxuries and many of the so-called comforts of life are not only dispensable, but positive hindrances to the elevation of mankind."[26]

To Thoreau, the establishment of the then-current form of American democracy was only a step towards the perfection of individualism, the very foundation of a better form of democracy that was in a state of becoming. He did not have a detailed dream of what the final product would be like. Instead, he welcomed the process of realizing an improved state of American democracy ignited only by the white hot energies of individualistic patriots pushing against the inertial deadweight of the existing government and resisting the drag of social traditions.

Thoreau put it like this: "Is a democracy, such as we know it, the last improvement possible in government? Is it not possible to take a step further towards recognizing and organizing the rights of man?"[27]

 Is a democracy, such as we know it, the last improvement possible in government? Is it not possible to take a step further towards recognizing and organizing the rights of man?"
Henry David Thoreau

Hoffman on the Continuing American Revolution

Hoffman, inspired by the perpetual motion machine we call the Continuing American Revolution, reinterpreted its reason-for-being in the context of the exuberance and psychoactivity of the 1960s. Consistent with his theory of politics-as-play and his tactical theories on capturing the attention of the mass media, his catchy epigram for this process was "Revolution for the Hell of It."

Beneath this veneer of bravado was a complexity of thought similar to that found in the more eloquent, weighty and oft-quoted tomes of Jefferson, Emerson and Thoreau. But, they thrived in an era of quills and elite dotage on literature. Hoffman was catapulted to public prominence in the age of a mass-appealing "boob tube." The technologies of communication have no small influence on the techniques of the communicator.

Resurrecting the political-existentialistic philosophy of

Thoreau in many ways, Hoffman dedicated himself lock, stock and barrel to being a modern standard-bearer of the Continuing American Revolution despite the costs. "I own no property, stocks, bonds or anything of substantial material value. It would not upset me so much were it not central to what I want to say, namely that we can live very well for much less than we are led to believe and still manage time to battle social or environmental injustices."[28]

I own no property, stocks, bonds or anything of substantial material value. It would not upset me so much were it not central to what I want to say, namely that we can live very well for much less than we are led to believe and still manage time to battle social or environmental injustices."

Abbie Hoffman

Combatting social and environmental pollution were two of Hoffman's commitments as a late-twentieth-century American everyday revolutionary. But true to the Libertarian genes in his complicated philosophy and the essence of Thoreau's philosophy, he also believed that the key to the American genetic code was individual personal liberty, particularly at this juncture in the history of the United States. Thus, it was incumbent on him to resist the accelerating encroachments against liberty and,

Injustice is transformed into justice only when people at critical points in their lives are willing to risk the consequences, go for freedom, and just say no."

Abbie Hoffman

thus, the erosion of the foundation of American democracy. "Injustice is transformed into justice only when people at critical points in their lives are willing to risk the consequences, go for freedom, and just say no."[29]

He understood, perhaps more than most of us, that this was a precarious undertaking, that the power of the "status quo" and the forces of reaction were not to be underrated. But, then, all his predecessors knew that being an infantryman in the Continuing American Revolution meant patrols, skirmishes, pitched battles, losses, retreats and regrouping. But there have been more than enough conquests throughout American history in which *liberty was triumphant,* e.g. The Bill of Rights, The Civil War, Woman's Suffrage, The Civil Rights Movement, to name a few. Better yet, these wins were cumulative (though not always immediate) and added up to a stronger democracy over the years. And playing even a minor role in these engagements had to have been a thrilling experience. "There is absolutely no greater high than challenging the power structure as a nobody, giving it your all, and winning."[30]

 There is absolutely no greater high than challenging the power structure as a nobody, giving it your all, and winning."
Abbie Hoffman

So Hoffman lived it out and lived it up as Emerson's "reformer, a remaker of what man has made," as Jefferson's medium for "a little rebellion, now and then," and as Thoreau's surrogate to help insure that this stage of American democracy was not "the last improvement possible in government."

Surgical Violence, Strategic Disobedience and Capturing The Flag

Making governmental improvements, working political reform and/or kindling rebellions are not a Sunday stroll on the beach. People who have power, who have "won" it by paying their political dues, do not yield it willingly, happily or (unless they must) peacefully. Governments have a monopoly on the legitimate use of force in society, and they have a strong notion to use it against those who try to wrench it from them.

This is not to say that all movements for major reform, uprisings and even "revolutions" in America have been greeted by the official deployment of lethal weaponry. True, the revolution against the British and the Civil War were gory affairs. On the other hand, major changes in American government brought about by outflanking the Articles of Confederation and through the agitation of the Progressive movement saw not one iota of blood spilled.

It is not surprising, then, that whether to employ violence as a means to bring about substantial political change in America has been the topic of much philosophizing. Those who favor nonviolence have a wide range of opinion. At one extreme is the absolute renunciation of any violence under any and all circumstances, i.e., not even defense of one's life. Those who follow this creed are the ultra-pacifists.

Somewhere in the middle is the position that one can "passively resist" government. This means that disobedients, protestors, and assorted rebels inject themselves into places from which government will eject them. They use their body weight to resist expulsion or arrest—which is a type of violence. Towards the other extreme are those who believe that sabotage against property, particularly that owned by government, is okay, as long as people are not injured.

At the far other extreme are those who profess all-out war to bring about revolutionary changes. This includes terrorism, guerrilla warfare and, if necessary, a clash of armies.

Abbie Hoffman had a ringside view of a goodly amount of bloodletting and ferocity during the civil disorders of the 1960s—and he was an unwilling and regular object of corporal punishment dished out by the police. So, he had a lot to say about it.

Philosophically he was a middle-of-the-roader. He was neither pacifist nor warrior, and he never advocated either of their positions in his philosophy. Nevertheless, in his capacity of political theorist, he saw some practical value in their thought and activities.

The most violence-choked action in which he participated was the Chicago "police riot" of 1968. Even at that time, Hoffman opposed the use of "indiscriminate" and "unstructured" violence by the counterculture—believing it was "suicidal." He was, however, a proponent of last-ditch self-defense against illegal police violence. He was also a proponent of what the U.S. military likes to call "surgical strikes," carefully targeting certain property for destruction, but going all out to avoid—again in official U.S. parlance—"collateral damage," i.e., injuring people. It was his view that those who held power needed to know that the opposition would and could resort to violence because "violence and the threat of violence have a good track record when it comes to changing the minds of the people in power"[31]

But, *he was 400 percent against terrorism*, not only because it was directed against human beings, but usually unarmed and innocent ones. "No one wins a revolution through hatred and intimidation of the general population. People are flesh and blood, not symbols. I agree with the notion that property has no inalienable rights; no revolution has occurred without destruction of property, especially symbols of power."[32]

 No one wins a revolution through hatred and intimidation of the general population. People are flesh and blood, not symbols. I agree with the notion that property has no inalienable rights; no revolution has ever occurred without the destruction of property, especially symbols of power."

Abbie Hoffman

Hoffman grew up in a lower-middle, working class family, with middle class morals and mores. Guns and smashface were alien to him, although he had to learn the manly art of self-defense. But he didn't reject violence against human beings solely because of class-based ethics. He was, first and foremost, a political realist and grasped what by now should be a truism: those who resort to terrorism (against or by the state) to inflict physical damage on innocent people are not worthy of political power!

If freedom, democracy, environmental protection, civil rights, and a government that is truly devoted to settling conflict by peaceful means (at home and abroad) are the goals, then killing, wounding or maiming other human beings is a sick, counterproductive and unforgivable way to attain it. "Not only is this kind of terrorism an unworkable strategy, it is one which could only replace one heartless system with another."[33]

 Not only is this kind of terrorism an unworkable strategy, it is one which could only replace one heartless system with another."
Abbie Hoffman

Later in his career, he came to believe that fighting the system by working completely out of it was a strategic and tactical error, "because it takes no brains to sit in or lie down and get carted off to jail."[34] He wasn't opposed to civil disobedience and passive resistance – but he came to favor a less conspicuous and passive balking at the oppression. His latter-day approach was to keep "one foot in the system," to discover ways and means to show the public that it is the government, or other power centers, who subvert the public good. He called this "capturing the flag" – long a successful tactic of right-wing activists. "Capturing the flag implies you are as good an American or better than the enforcers."[35]

 Capturing the flag implies you are as good an American or better than the enforcers."
Abbie Hoffman

Hoffman saw this strategy as an effective complement to civil disobedience and surgical violence (outsider tactics). *Being partly inside helps one learn the strengths and weaknesses of the system and provides a strategic position from which to reveal the true nature of its operation. Being one-half in the system, using guile to evade and subvert its oppressive techniques, and using the media to expose the truth are elements of what might be called strategic disobedience.*

The mature Hoffman would have given four-star reviews to outsider civil disobedience media events like the ocean interventions of the Greenpeace Warrior. He would have lauded radical environmentalists who sit in trees about to be logged and those who drive nails into precious redwoods to prevent them from being chainsawed (so long as they tell the loggers and the sawmill operators what they have done to avoid collateral damage). Here we have imaginative, graphic, media-friendly tactics of civil disobedience. Moreover, they are focused on and limited to obstructing business-as-usual and highly specific property destruction that is successful in getting the public to pay attention to and understand their crusades. These are major components of Hoffman's ideas about "participatory media tactics"—one of his fortes.

Participatory Media Tactics: Awakening and Involving the Public Mind

As we have seen, Abbie Hoffman staked out a place for himself alongside some great American philosophers, reinventing ideas similar to theirs, but with a late twentieth-century flair. He did, however, carve out a special niche for himself through his extensive theorizing and intensive experimenting with unorthodox mass media maneuvers to awaken the American people to an alternative reality.

It was obvious to Hoffman, that few in the modern American transformational movement had even the foggiest hint of how the media worked. They were antagonistic to it, tried to ignore it, and thus were largely victimized by it.

> 'The movement' is not serious about the right thing. It attacks the media because it is controlled by the ruling class. Sure that's true. But activists have to learn how it works. Ninety percent of peace activists I meet have less knowledge about how (as opposed to why) the media works than does any junior executive in an ad agency.[36]

Hoffman put a lot of his thought as a modern media tactician into print. The part we will emphasize here is what we see as its nucleus, a way to achieve largely democratic goals with participatory media tactics that do not lecture or proselytize. Instead, his tactics empower the public to discover and define its own original view of political realities by provoking people's minds.

This man-child of the TV age was a genius at manipulating imagery. He was a pioneer at rearranging images so as to deconstruct false visions and defy the pseudo-consciousness created by those in control of the media. The purpose was to get people (the mass television, radio and newsprint audiences) to (a) become alert to the fact that they were being brainwashed, (b) learn new ways to look at TV, (c) become more open to clearly

 'The Movement' is not serious about the right thing. It attacks the media because it is controlled by the ruling class. Sure that's true. But activists have to learn how it works. Ninety percent of peace activists I meet have less knowledge about how (as opposed to why) the media works than does any junior executive in an ad agency."

Abbie Hoffman

off-center ideas he managed to infiltrate through the dimly flickering screen.

Hoffman was ingenious at inducing the public into involvement, sometimes against its will. His instrument was shock — jolting people into occupying a position alien to themselves, even if only momentarily. This programed them so they might be able to read the official TV menu differently. If they realized they were being fed bland mush, and got a whiff of a savory filet mignon, they might subsequently accept a plan on how they could sink their teeth into some steak. They might start to think differently and, hopefully, act differently.

The key, as usual, was in splicing together democracy, the continuing spirit of the American revolution, and individual, but intensely public freedom. This was one reason why he adopted "Free" as one of his favorite alter egos. "The Yippie political program was built around FREE, and by using the word as my pseudonym I wanted to say that the individual is not separate from his or her politics."[37]

Many political writers during American revolutionary times used Latin pen-names to connect them to ancient ideas, classical times. Abbie Hoffman used names that expressed aspects of his ideas about the joys of individual liberation— "Free," "Yippie!"

 The Yippie political program was built around *free*, and by using the word as my pseudonym I wanted to say that the individual is not separate from his or her politics."

Abbie Hoffman

Hoffman was relentless in crafting a wide variety of media needles by which to puncture the illusion of an independent, professional and objective press. It was this myth which he believed kept citizens chained to their TV sets, to a phony politics, and to a distorted and perverted set of priorities dangerous to the common health and commonwealth.

To dispel the media myth he discussed, devised, divined and developed multiple methods of converting all his media opportunities into political consciousness-raising. No matter how freakish the episode, how weird the gig, how offbeat the practical joke—it was usually designed, rehearsed and refined to achieve the same goal: Wake up! Be Free! Get Involved! "The goal of this nameless art form—part vaudeville, part insurrection, part communal recreation—was to shatter the pretense of objectivity."[38]

 The goal of this nameless art form—part vaudeville, part insurrection, part communal recreation—was to shatter the pretense of objectivity."

Abbie Hoffman

Hoffman studied the media, understood how well it works, and then orchestrated totally unexpected scenarios to catch the media off guard—to reveal their bias, the reality of their means of mastery. On TV, one had to bait the TV talk show host, so he or she might lose his or her composure. Or one might set up a situation that appears to be censorship by the TV station, for example, by silently mouthing obscenities ("Oh my God . . . they blipped him right there! I saw it!").[39]

In the major national newsmagazines, many readers start to read from the back because they are more interested in items about entertainment, people, and styles, than they are about "hard" news. So, Hoffman gained initial media access through a "back door" approach, a wily way of luring media attention by some newfangled lifestyle, fashion, fad, contraption, or event. Once having established a media aura, either as a person or group, one finds it easier to gain access, or work one's way up, to the more "serious" sections. This was the fundamental theory behind developing "media events" and "guerrilla" or "street theatre"—his brand of stand-up and low-down political satire. The method and theory to the media madness was to capture the public eye, captivate the public imagination, and pump life into a politically moribund public. If it were left exclusively up to media "pros" to report alternative political messages, the epidemic of brain-deadening would continue to spread.

However, media events and guerilla theatre were participatory at both ends. The "actors" made up their own roles, directed their own scenes. Success was calibrated by the extent to which others were enlightened, "turned on," or jarred out of their complacency.

In prepping for these performances, the players would settle into groups to plan some of the more complicated enterprises or psyche themselves and others up for upcoming "free-for-all be-ins." These were meant to be spontaneous outlets for massive protests or expressions of counterculture values. Whatever the type of gathering and action, it was of utmost importance to let the structure and content evolve, *particularly in the minds of those who would witness it*: "If observers of the drama are allowed to interpret the act, they will become participants themselves. Too much analysis kills direct theatrical experience . . . . The concept of mass spectacle, every-day language, and easily recognized symbols was important to get public involvement."[40]

Yes, whatever the method, one had to respect the power of language, its ability to reach John and Jane Doe in whatever medium was used. The idea he expressed repeatedly—as if to make verbal exclamation points—was to reach out and touch the public so they could understand quickly and easily!!!!!

 If observers of the drama are allowed to interpret the act, they will become participants themselves. Too much analysis kills direct theatrical experience. . . . The concept of Mass spectacle, every-day language, and easily recognized symbols was important to get public involvement."

Abbie Hoffman

Language should be action-oriented, exciting, creative, simple and upbeat. *Try to imagine yourself as someone creating an advertising campaign.* Activists who carry around some prejudice that all advertising is deceitful, who feel that emphasizing form threatens the integrity of content really miss the essential nature of communication. *You can't afford the luxury of being boring or of creating a language that the average person cannot understand.*[41]

Of and Beyond His Time: Hoffman's Transformational Philosophy

As we have indicated before, all political philosophies are a reflection of their times, as well as a personalized projection of a future for which they yearn. So Hoffman's is starkly unlike any previous American political philosophy. After all, the America his philosophy mirrors is radically unlike any preceding our present-day model.

Of course, as we have also noted, the bedrock themes in Hoffman's philosophy have powerful ties to traditional American political philosophical writing. The values he embraced and the general path he wanted to see America travel, in years to come, are in sync with perennial American themes.

What is more, the tales of despair and disgust he narrates are not all that different from the general view of the severe problems in American culture depicted by philosophers past: inequality of wealth, widespread poverty, over-control by government, expansive militarism, an apathetic public, venal politicians, a jingoistic press, a hypocritical society, oppression of ethnic and racial minorities, and so on. None of this is fresh fuel to feed the fires of philosophical discontent and all of it can be found dappled through Hoffman's work.

But regard the differences! The ways this man elected to present his philosophy were — to say the least — unconventional and if we may coin a word here, downright *unphilosophical*. Next, many topics he selected to focus on represent a society in massive "future shock,"[42] one having, and that will continue to have, great difficulties in coming to terms with rapidly altering and startlingly unprecedented challenges. Each of these steadily erupting crises are unique in American history, but the sum of them is mind blasting.

The accelerating transformation of American culture and society is now the mode. Both the style and substance of Hoffman's philosophy are a product of this. Together they represent his contribution to what he saw as the *sine qua non* to completing the next evolutionary step in American democracy: checkmating the reaction against these changes and elevating the American political system onto its next higher plane.

Hoffman's Transformational Style

Marshall McLuhan, an influential analyst of the media during the 1960s, said *The Medium is the Massage*, which was often misinterpreted and even more widely recited as the medium is the *message*.[43] In other words, how a missive was transmitted, was at least as important (if not more important) than the material in it. Hoffman illustrated this in the way he offered up his philosophy — whether as a guest on a TV show, as a pamphleteer, or as an author.

Reading his books is otherworldly, an experience unlike reading Jefferson, Thoreau, Emerson or Dewey. His philosophy is not systematically presented, with one idea logically following another. Unlike his predecessors, Hoffman's written work caters to an "unsophisticated" readership — teenagers, dropouts, mind astronauts, among others. Each book is a first-person "trip" of one kind or another. And that's both the message *and* the massage.

Much of Hoffman's writing is an autobiographical journey, chronicling his adventures and misadventures. There's lots of personal grist in them, wisecracks, opinions about voyaging on Spaceship Earth. Sprinkled occasionally in this box of verbal crackerjacks are prizes, that which is of value to the cortex plus political guides to what should be done. These tidbits are the essence of his substantive philosophy. But caution: it is the medium that is the message!

As we have emphasized throughout, to Hoffman the process of getting there is more than half the game. *Living a life informed and led by a democratic political philosophy is the message. The medium is: Have fun. Live a full life. Be yourself. Try hard to relate to all God's children. Be Free. Be hooked on people, not status or property. Don't try to be too logical. Bounce around a lot. Don't be afraid to be different and challenge the norm. Being outrageous has positive values, but be willing to take the lumps.*

This was the style of most of his books. Like his political actions and his personal life, they are in direct contradiction to the kind of social and political values that Hoffman jabbed and poked at his whole life. He believed that hierarchy and uniformity were hardening the arteries of the American body politic — and worse yet, the heart of the American people. People were becoming too comfortable in what was usual, in positions they already held, and in ideas that were not only antiquated, but diametrically opposite to their own interests.

They needed to be liberated from these shackles or else American liberty and democracy would be swallowed up and replaced by a lifeless patriotic pomp, posturing, and postulation — words posing as ideas, devoid of mental vitality. Hoffman's lifestyle, his style of writing and his political philosophy were brandished as a sword against the forces of autocracy, authoritarianism, regimentation and anti-democracy.

Hoffman was and remains something truly nonpareil, a one-of-a-kind on the American political philosophical scene. He understood that the contemporary technological background, the present political scene, the contemporary political non-critique and the way all this is dispatched to the eye of the American public was beyond anything his forerunners could ever imagine. An astonishing new way to counteract it had to be invented. Hoffman did that. The political medium was the political message and the message had everything to do with the politics of modern media.

Hoffman's Transformational Philosophy

The 1960s were a truly remarkable time in American history. They were years of overt resistance to overseas military adventurism; mushrooming citizen alienation from government; uncommon civil rights demonstrations; the genesis of a new feminism; the insemination of the modern environmental movement; and a multi-frontal assault on the bastions of many traditional American social values, including: education, sexual mores, nutritional and clothing habits, means to artificially alter consciousness, etc.

Whether coincidental, or correlated with some invisible subterranean socio-economic-political force, all this massive upheaval within a short time frame triggered a tidal wave of change. Although the same sense of chaotic disruption that accompanied the apparent coincidence of these movements as a united "counterculture" does not exist today, each movement continues its own part of the struggle for a radical metamorphosis in the American way at home and abroad.

This presently disjointed transformational movement has had its share of wins and losses. African-Americans have scored heavily in their eternal contest for social, political and economic parity in America. Yet, in other ways, the tally is worse than before the Watts riot in 1965. Deep racism lingers, albeit in ever more subtle ways. Tokenism and affirmative action help in making America's image less racist, but also create backlashes that reverse some gains and sap or sidetrack scarce resources.

The women's rights movement has also won some big battles since the publication of Betty Friedan's *The Feminist Mystique* in 1963.[44] This social revolution has come a long way since then, with women being integrated into America's economic and social life in ways and to degrees hardly imagined a few decades ago. But, they remain far short of a fair shake almost everywhere, with American women bumping their heads on "glass ceilings" in every institutional setting in 1990s American society.

The new environmental movement has picked up lots of steam in the past score of years. Through its Herculean efforts, concepts like the greenhouse effect, holes in the ozone layer, recycling, toxic waste dumps, and a host of others, have become household words and phrases. Even some gigantic multinational corporations, who number among the most flagrant contaminators, have developed some scruples about their generous contributions to the degradation of the biosphere and atmosphere. But this movement, too, senses it is running up a down escalator. Change in position is slow despite tremendous expenditures of energy. There are too many cavernous loopholes in environment-friendly legislation and brigades of overpaid lawyers who know how to drive foul-smelling trucks through them. Worse still, national mandates don't have sufficient reach to address global problems.

The peace and conflict resolution movements were buoyed by their success in hastening the withdrawal of American forces from Vietnam and by the prospects of a "peace dividend" flowing from what everyone hopes is the end (or continued winding down) of the Cold War. They were sobered, however, by a resurgence of American militarism in the wake of President Bush's thrust towards "the new world order." The outpouring of "triumphalism" spurred by the rout of Saddam Hussein's armies in Kuwait and Iraq in 1991 stunted the growth of the movement which favors peaceful negotiation, mediation, cooperation and collaboration. Conversely, the crisis in the Persian Gulf glorified war as a solution to complicated, sensitive international issues. It also oiled the mechanism for siphoning precious capital into increasingly exotic, esoteric and expensive military hardware and software. America's social and economic infrastructure problems would probably have to wait in line again.

Those who crusaded for a new kind of American democracy over the past two decades have also been stalemated. The defection of American voters from national elections has continued — and will continue at least until 1992.

Only half the eligible electorate votes in presidential elections and slightly more than a third votes for Congress. Furthermore, Political Action Committees (PACs) of huge, organized interests dominate the legislative, executive and administrative processes. But attempts to implement new forms of participatory democracy have received scant support at either the federal, state or local levels or from private sources. The only place that *new* applications of participatory democracy seem to be making real headway in America is in a few businesses and industries who are experimenting with workplace democracy. The impetus for these, however, is the ominously burgeoning threat of the Japanese economy and the fact that much of Japan's success is due to its use of worker participation processes in major industrial production.

So what has all this to do with Abbie Hoffman and his philosophy for a free and green America? We believe the crux of why all these movements have not begun to approach their full promise is that most of the well-meaning, hardworking, altruistic, and devoted people who support them are *insulated* in their thought and action. They are *isolated* from a multitude of natural allies. They are *sequestered* from the public support they crave and fail to tap. They seem to be uncomprehending of the underlying, extensive and interconnected nature of the problem and how to team up to combat it.

Notice that Hoffman's existence, his political agitation and cogitation, touched and was touched by *all* these movements — from his initial sally as an activist to his dying day. He took part in black voting rights activities in Mississippi in the early 1960s. He was a major cog in the anti-war movement in the late 1960s. He was an environmental activist even as a hunted fugitive in the 1970s. He fought for personal liberty and for private individuals in the War on Drugs during the 1980s. He evangelized for democratic reform throughout his lifetime. Although he was properly attacked by feminists for gender insensitivity (if not "womanizing") in his youth, he repented for such and came to appreciate and promote feminism and gender equality later in his life.

This is not meant to be a eulogy for Abbie Hoffman, renaissance radical. It is simply to observe and emphasize that all these movements were a salient part of Hoffman's life as well as of his political philosophy. He was not a restless political hobo, hopping frantically from one political train to another. Instead, his philosophy had sufficient density and gravity to pull each movement into his orbit. So, when opportunities arose for him to contribute to each of them, it was not only consistent, but imperative, for him to do so, and they benefitted by his presence.

What is needed, then, is a political philosophy for our times, one that can bond these separate movements together in some way that they may better synergize into a cooperative, transformational coalition. We think Hoffman's qualifies.

Abbie, the Green?

There is another political philosophy that might also qualify, one similar in many ways to Hoffman's and one that may serve as the ideological underpinning for a consolidated political movement. This is the political philosophy of the Green parties and the Green movements in several countries in the world, including the United States.

Greens in Europe are popularly known (at least in America) as "environmentalists." Much of their media notoriety has come from helping put environmental concerns, if not deep ecological thought, higher on the political agenda of establishment parties and politics. If nothing else, some of the Green environmental program has been coopted by majoritarian politics and has had and will continue to have a salutary, but limited, impact.

The Green agenda, though, has much more substance at its epicenter. Other key Green principles are: (1) opposition to militarism and violent means to resolve domestic and international conflicts—with substantial opposition to nuclear power, (2) what they call "post-patriarchal values," (3) grassroots democracy and decentralization of governmental and economic power, (4) respect for diversity of cultural differences. Sounds familiar by now, doesn't it?

In other words, the Green philosophy and its democratic organizational principles seem to dovetail nicely with those of Abbie Hoffman. So why don't we just declare Abbie Hoffman an ancestor of the American Greens, let the Greens acknowledge him as an American proponent of their philosophy, and call it quits?

There are several reasons. First, many (if not most) Greens would think that Hoffman's philosophy isn't quite as seasoned and profound, in some respects, as their own. In other ways, they would either dispute his ideas or consider them unwise. Second, Hoffman's work includes some major points absent in the Green philosophy, decisive elements that distance his thinking from that of the American Greens.

Although Hoffman did considerable work in environmental groups and on environmental issues, the Greens' philosophy covers a lot more ground than protecting a river here and there from the Army Corps of Engineers or upstream despoilers. The Green program speaks, instead, of promoting nothing less than "ecological wisdom." By this, they embrace the systemic thinking expressed in James Lovelock's "Gaia Hypothesis,"[45] which is close to the outlook lived by Native Americans before they were uprooted, downgraded, sideswiped and dispossessed by Western civilization.

In this view, the earth's elements and all creatures who dwell upon and within it are intertwined and interdependent. Planet Earth, itself, is a mammoth living organism. In order for it to thrive and/or survive, it must maintain an eco-balance. But humankind, particularly the U.S.A., is speeding along a hazardous superhighway, on its way to mortally disrupting that equilibrium and causing irreversible damage to nature's ability to regenerate. America is using itself up, degenerating, because people have little sense of harmony among themselves, with their work, and with their natural environs.

Actually, Hoffman vibrated to this worldview. During his flight from prosecution, he visited a secluded town in the mountains of New Mexico. It was populated, in the main, by a tiny cluster of emigres who fled the industrialized/commercial/ bureaucratized society of urban, suburban and exurban America. He resided there for a short while but soon came to admire the way they combined their pioneering way of life with an entrepreneurial spirit, a sense of community, a love of family, and an understanding of how to manipulate bureaucracy. He was impressed by the sensitive way they wove together their social values, their political philosophy, and their caring attitude toward their harsh and sparse natural setting:

> What then keeps the people here? Mostly it's the other people. People with strong ideas on matters like ecology. Almost every family uses recycled water, is experimenting with solar energy, and tries their luck at organic gardening. It's a highly educated group that dreads specialization. Enough so to force themselves to learn carpentry, mechanics, irrigation, and a host of other manual skills. In addition, they've had to educate themselves in the ways of the paper jungle. Learning everything there was to know about water rights, township charters, federal and state assistance programs. They're a people content to work in the hotels and restaurants of Santa Fe or start a small pottery business and put a good hunk of their energy into the community and the land.[46]

In describing his fight to help conserve the St. Lawrence River, he spoke of Indian ways in that area, and of the strong interrelationships between the natural environment, the native wildlife, the indigenous beauty of the place and the peril to it from those who would demolish its symmetry for small-minded, large-scale economic gains. Although not a great ecologist or ecological philosopher, his philosophy incorporates much of the Green ideal of ecological wisdom.

Hoffman also came to see a relationship between American military excursions abroad and massive damage to global ecology—long before the label "ecoterrorism" was attached to the evil escapades of Saddam Hussein in the Persian Gulf. Even such attacks on the environment like the torching of Kuwait's oil fields or the U.S. Army defoliating whole Vietnamese jungles with Agent Orange were not the worst kind of assault from Hoffman's point of view. It went further than that. What he saw was the use of imperialistic armed might to capture, pillage, loot and strip the earth (above and below) of its bounty—for the overconsumption by a rapacious, small percentage of the world's population (the U.S.A.). To Abbie Hoffman, later and deeper in this thoughts, *all* wars became "ecology wars." In his words, " . . . I've been rethinking that the war in Vietnam, the genocidal wars against the Indians, all wars in fact, are ecology wars. They're attempts to take the land and natural resources that belong to all the people of the planet and concentrate them for the energy and the consumption and the greed of the few."[47]

> . . . I've been rethinking that the war in Vietnam, the genocidal wars against the Indians, all wars in fact, are ecology wars. They're attempts to take the land and the natural resources that belong to all of the people of the planet and concentrate them for the energy and the consumption and the greed of the few."
> *Abbie Hoffman*

Although Hoffman leaned towards gender equality later in his life, from what can be found in his writings, he does not seem to have appreciated fully the Green principle of "post-patriarchal values."

This Green tenet requires a lot more than filling a hiring quota for women or asking men to share the household chores. It is part of a deeper critique of male-dominated society, where masculine logic, aggressiveness, competition, and brashness are highly esteemed and rewarded. In a society beyond this retarded stage, feminine characteristics such as nurturing, listening, cooperativeness and modesty must be highly valued and widely practiced by men as well as women.

Hoffman's later work began to address these issues, but even while trying to grasp and laud the eco-feminist approach, he still oversimplified it. For instance, while waxing eloquent over progress along these lines, he described the women's movement as a "healthy step up the human ladder."[48] But, from his still somewhat premature perspective, this ascension consisted mainly of equalizing societal roles and ironing out sexual relationships. How he actually developed his relationships with the women in his life is at best implicit in his writing. Anyone calling himself a "macho-feminist,"[49] however, definitely had not yet reached the periphery or depth of Green post-patriarchy.

Another gap between the thinking of Hoffman, the American political philosopher, and that of the American Greens would appear to be in his views on how movements, and any organizations within movements, should be run internally. Although a strong proponent of democracy, Hoffman came to gag on the theory and practice of consensual democracy. The American Greens, at least up to the present time, are ideologically committed to deciding everything by consensus, that is, everyone must agree (sometimes "everyone" is defined as 90%, 80%, or thereabouts). The process by which this is accomplished is not the rigid Roberts Rules of Order. Instead, unanimity is reached by an extremely informal process conducted by mediation and facilitation.

Hoffman's experiences with the counterculture of the 1960s and 1970s had turned him into an implacable foe of consensualism. In fact, he HATED it, seeing it as an albatross around the neck of change: "In the sixties we always made decisions by

> **❝ In the sixties we always made decisions by consensus. By 1970, when you had 15 people show up and three were FBI agents and six were schizophrenics, universal agreement was getting to be a problem. I call it 'The curse of consensus decision making,' because in the end consensus decision making is rule by the minority, the easiest form to manipulate, the easiest way to block any real decision making."**
> **Abbie Hoffman**

consensus. By 1970, when you had 15 people show up and three were FBI agents and six were schizophrenics, universal agreement was getting to be a problem. I call it 'The Curse of Consensus Decision Making,' because in the end consensus decision making is rule by the minority, the easiest form to manipulate, the easiest way to block any real decision making."[50]

Ironically, he came to appreciate some of the finer points in the rule-by-majority model. Why? Because, from his experience over the years, it was "the toughest to stack." He saw it as forcing different sides on an issue to "get cooperation, and to go out and get more people to come in to have those votes the next time around."[51]

Hoffman's philosophy, as we have seen, also includes a great deal of theorizing about wresting the power of modern media technology and techniques from those who preempt it. This is essential for the new American political transformational process to continue to grow and eventually succeed. Various parts of the transformational movement, including the civil rights movement, the women's rights movement, the environmental movement and the peace movement have fathomed this and utilized it successfully every so often. The Greens have not fared as well. They don't understand the value in and art of manipulating the mass media to get their message across. This prevents them from being able to educate, alert and involve the American public in their complex and self-sacrificing transformational ideas and goals. Hoffman observed: "It just seems stupid to me that people who want to create a revolution can avoid trying to master the most revolutionary means of communication since language itself was created."[52]

Unfortunately, though, at this point in time, the Greens and the entire transformational movement seem stalled in their attempt to gain power, whether through established institutions or by persuading the public through the mass media. Whatever power base remains in the movement is mainly in the minds and actions of individuals and in scattered ventures of local groups and uncoordinated moves by national organizations.

Perhaps the biggest disparity between Hoffman, the Green philosophy and the various and sundry parts of the transformational movement comes in the explicit value Hoffman places on personal liberty and the role of the individual in transformational politics. One might imply a value of individualism from the Green advocacy of "respect for diversity," "grassroots democracy" and consensual politics, but not much. Their focus is narrowed to specific issues like racial or gender fairness, or ecological balance. Individualism is at best a marginal concern. The rest of the transformational movement pays scant attention to it as well. For Hoffman, though, it was the very heart of the matter, the wellspring of his thinking. It was a new slant on

good old American individualism, to be sure, but an elaboration
and improvement on American individualism nevertheless.

Abbie, The American Evolutionary

Hoffman participated in many transformational organizations, but we think it is fair to say that he never "belonged" to
any. When he worked in and for one, he was always a leading
role player, a primal energy source. But he was emphatically
not an "organization man." He had a healthy distrust of most
"leaders," even though American culture, political circumstances, the media and some compatriots would compel him to
acknowledge others as leaders and to perform as one from time
to time.

Hoffman knew that people had to "organize" to accomplish
immediate, intermediate, and remote political goals, and he
was a master of that. Still, there is nothing in his writing to sug-
gest that he believed that transformational change in America
would be worked by any kind of centralized national organization, and certainly not by a third party, which he felt was
"futile."

He was a movement man — but not a parochial one. He supported, sweated and bled for many parts of the major transformational movement (civil rights, peace, environmental). Each
part of the movement was nourished by the labor of individuals,
local organizations, ad hoc groups, support networks, and di-
verse national organizations. He saw and supported the need
and utility of all these for progress to be made. But the quark of
the entire transformational movement, and its subparts, is: the
transformational individual. It is the informed and radicalized
individual citizen in which Hoffman had the greatest hope and
faith.

We've already mentioned several negative tendencies that
Hoffman saw in these movements, patterns that prevented them
from attaining greater success for their own cause and in collaboration with allied movements (including self-isolation, media illiteracy, and effective subversion by government). But
there were other major reasons why Hoffman was not eager to

stick around any particular transformational organization for too long.

The social glue that unites most anti-establishment associations is a sense of moral superiority and ideological purity (it most assuredly isn't the pursuit of material success). The problem is that these attitudes all too frequently deteriorate into an overbearing and underachieving snobbery and pomposity — often aimed at *insiders*, mostly volunteers. Here's how Hoffman put it:

> We should stop demanding that we all become instant saints and be more tolerant of our comrades, especially if they are active. The cultism of the left often appears as three people, two of whom plot to kick the third out. It's always because of another *ism*. Sexism, racism, elit*ism*, deviational*ism*. I'd rather see people kicked out because they don't follow through on their commitment. . . . But deviate from the manners or the vocabulary of the party line and out you go. That's sick to me and self-defeating.[53]

 We should stop demanding that we all become instant saints and be more tolerant of our comrades, especially if they are active. The cultism of the left often appears as three people, two of whom plot to kick the third out. It's always because of another *ism*. Sexism, racism, elit*ism*, deviational*ism*. I'd rather see people kicked out because they don't follow through on their commitment. . . . But deviate from the manners or the vocabulary of the party line and out you go. That's sick to me and self-defeating."

Abbie Hoffman

Another harmful glitch in movement politics that annoyed and frustrated Hoffman was the super-earnestness and deadly seriousness of its practitioners. Being intense and grimly determined is their way to charge and recharge batteries. Worse yet, true believers, even when they try to let their hair down, lack the kind of spontaneous humor and wild and crazy ideas that he believed were necessary to help grease the skids to a popularly based transformation. Just as terrorism turned the public off, so did the paradox of a somber "new" politics.

These ideas did not (and still don't) sit too well with many in the transformational movement—whether of the old or new schools. "The use of fun in struggle was a new notion . . . . There's no incongruity in conducting serious business and having fun. This pissed off the straight left no end."[54] So, in order to keep his spirits up and his juices flowing, he zigzagged through many groups and groupings, offering his ideas, help and efforts, but he always moved on.

 The use of fun in struggle was a new notion. . . . There's no incongruity in conducting serious business and having fun. This pissed off the straight left no end."
                                                    Abbie Hoffman

Thus, Abbie Hoffman was in and out, here and there, betwixt and between. The basic unit of his political transformational philosophy was the patriotic individual, committed to the Continuing American Revolution: a self-propelled, inner-directed, self-actualizing, perpetually mutating, self-correcting, high-spirited, good-humored, humanly and humanely interactive ball of energy.

Hoffman's life is an odyssey of one man's daring passage through and contributions to many modern American transformational movements and organizations. It is an epic poem with countless lessons for those who bear witness to it. *Hoffman's individualistic, public-spirited political philosophy is worthy of respect by any who want to help integrate the existing forces for change and evolutionize America into the twenty-first century.* It is a lot Left, some Right, a great deal Green—the sum total of which is genuine, industrial-strength Hoffman.

What follows is a thumbnail recap of this philosophy which may be useful in defining the reader's role in how to help American society transform itself into one that is more free, more ecologically wise, more democratic, more American.

[A]. The chief problems are — as outlined before — the snowballing tendencies towards corporate monopolism and a bureaucratic, militarized state that tries to (1) shrink individual freedom; (2) isolate and stratify individuals through procreating false consciousness; and (3) exploit individuals and the local, national and global environment in order to make excessive profits.

[B]. Patriotic citizens can best deal with these menaces by (1) studying the intricate nature and symptoms of the socio-economic-political-ecological problem; (2) analyzing how it impacts on them personally; (3) striving personally to resist or help solve any and all aspects of the problem when an opportunity presents itself politically, at work, at play or at home.

[C]. Although the individual citizen is the driving force behind American democracy, the turbine of democratic transformational change, Hoffman's individualism is not the atomistic, ego-maniacal one of Ayn Rand and most "objectivists." It is a new interactive and politically transcendent kind, one that appreciates, upholds and compromises with the rights and liberties of all people and accommodates the natural environment as well.[55] Thus, she or he must learn to cooperate with and actively support the individuality of others and Gaia — as long as they don't use force against her or him.

[D]. Major transformational change can best come through helping manufacture changes in the collective American consciousness. Organizations can, through independent or interdependent efforts, help facilitate some transformation of the American psyche, particularly through innovative and creative uses of the mass media. A large portion of this will come in how they engage the establishment in the streets, the fields, the courts, the schools, on TV, in print. National organizations can also help those working individually and locally feel that they are part of something bigger and more important than their own personal and local preoccupations.

[E]. Whatever part or parts of the problem one chooses to grapple with, she or he should strive to be nonviolent towards other persons and be as passively resistant to the use of force against them as humanly possible. People in the movement must also learn to indulge the deficiencies of others in the movement, as well as the general public, and not be supercilious, sanctimonious or self-righteous. No one is perfect. They must try as hard as they can to bite their tongues, be emotionally supportive and lead by personal example.

[F]. Individuals must learn about, promote and fight for a greater American democracy in all aspects of her or his life. This means opposing hierarchies at home, at work and in government and politics. A new type of leadership that consults with and listens to the people is required. There must be more and new ways of direct citizen, worker and family involvement.

[G]. Another weighty canon in Hoffman's Law is: experience pleasure while doing all this. If it stops being enjoyable, stop doing it. Remember that there is no end to the Continuing American Revolution and that even though each person is essential, no one is indispensable to its inevitable success. So even when things are not going well, they will eventually— even if you are not around. Fancy the process. Otherwise, you'll become part of the old politics and part of the problem. You'll also burn out sooner than later.

It's tough enough to be true to such an intricate and taxing philosophy in one's own life. It sure took its toll on Abbie Hoffman. But by immersing one's self in the attempt to act out this philosophy, she or he adds her or his singular light to the continuing spirit of the American Revolution. It's out of the question to expect any massive, national organization to do so alone. National transformation will not come exclusively via any national organization. It will occur only when a critical mass of enlightened and personally transformed individuals fuse into an irresistible force. The result is likely to be the next evolutionary period in American democracy.

What humankind has learned in the latter part of the twentieth century is that highly centralized, totalitarian states— Marxist or Capitalist—tremble and implode when confronted by an undaunted, peaceful citizenry who rise up *en masse* to dismantle the system or demand it change its heart and soul.

The Shah of Iran's mighty army and diabolical secret police folded their tents quickly and quietly when braved by an army of their fellow Iranian citizens brandishing banners, signs and chains — with which they beat *themselves!* The brutal dictator Ferdinand Marcos jetted to Hawaii when his malicious military machine was swamped by a sea of peaceful Filipino demonstrators demanding "people power." The Polish and East German Communist Parties, honor graduates of the Genghis Khan School of Government, were cowed by the roar of millions of protesters — never firing a shot in defense of their power. Colossal bureaucracies of tyranny dissolved almost overnight with a whimper, not even a bang.

The American system of corporate centralism and governmental oligarchy is much more shrewd, sophisticated and resilient than any and all of the above. It benefits by, but is also vulnerable to, the brilliance of the American Constitution and the power of traditional American political values. No matter how invulnerable and immutable the system may seem, when the time comes, it will fail to thwart the nonviolent transformational ultimatums issued by tens of millions of Americans.

No one can tell when the next major step in American democracy's evolution to a higher plane will come to pass, or what peculiar shape it will take. All we know is that it will eventuate some time in the future, because such gains are inexorable in American history. *This, not making millions of dollars, is the real American Dream.*

Many Americans who lived political philosophies dedicated to the elimination of slavery, or to making women the political equals of men, died well before these laudable goals were achieved. They may not have been alive to see their political fantasy materialized, but their lives and deaths were not in vain. They took part in the drawn out, troublesome, sometimes painful, but always spiritually rewarding process of democratic reform in this nation. Their powers, talents and sacrifices were not squandered.

Abbie Hoffman did not live to see the kind and degree of change in American society that he longed for, and he probably lost heart of seeing it in his lifetime. He did leave behind a philosophy, though, one that he, like any philosopher, had trouble living up to.

We believe that his philosophy will long outlive his reputation and deeds as a political satirist, political organizer and media celebrity. He lives on, in his books and in this one. His ultimate influence in helping evolve the kind of America he envisioned and championed will in part depend on the number of Americans who try, as hard as they can, to *Live This Book*.

Notes

Part I. Abbie Hoffman: American Satirist, Theorist and Philosopher

1. Abbie Hoffman, *Soon to be a Major Motion Picture* (New York: G.P. Putnam Sons, 1980), 102.

2. Mark Twain, vol. 1 of *Following The Equator* (New York: Harper & Brothers, 1899), 98.

3. Frederick Anderson, ed., *A Pen Warmed-up in Hell: Mark Twain in Protest* (New York: Harper and Row, 1971), 4.

4. Ibid., p. 91.

5. Ibid., p. xviii.

6. Ibid., p. 18.

7. Richard M. Ketchum, *Will Rogers: The Man and His Times* (New York: Simon and Schuster, 1973), 151, (emphasis ours).

8. Ibid., p. 317.

9. Ibid., p. 336.

10. William R. Brown, *Imagemaker: Will Rogers and the American Dream* (Columbia, MO: University of Missouri Press, 1970), 131.

11. Charles Chaplin, *My Autobiography* (New York: Simon and Schuster, 1964), 391.

12. Ibid., p. 470.

13. Quoted in David Robinson, *Chaplin: The Mirror of Opinion* (Bloomington, IN: Indiana University Press, 1983), 95.

14. Chaplin, *My Autobiography*, p. 468.

15. Thomas Hobbes, *Leviathan*, edited by Francis B. Randall (New York: Washington Square Press, 1964), 85.

16. Thucydides 2.40.2, translated by Rex Warner, as quoted in Cecil M. Bowra, *Periclean Athens* (New York: The Dial Press, 1971), 129.

17. Theodore J. Lowi and Benjamin Ginsberg, *American Govern-*

ment: *Freedom and Power* (New York: W.W. Norton and Company, 1990), 33.

18. Theodore L. Becker, "Conflict and Paradox in the New American Mediation Movement: Status Quo and Social Transformation," *Missouri Journal of Dispute Resolution*. 1986, p. 129.

19. Arthur M. Schlesinger, Jr., *The Cycles of American History* (Boston: Houghton Mifflin Company, 1986).

20. Ibid., p. 23.

21. Ibid., p. 24.

22. Ibid., p. 47.

Part II. Elements of Hoffman's Philosophy: What's Wrong With America

1. C. Wright Mills, *The Power Elite* (New York: Oxford University Press, 1956).

2. G. William Domhoff, *Who Rules America* (Englewood Cliffs, NJ: Prentice-Hall, 1967).

3. Edward S. Greenberg, *Serving the Few* (New York: Wiley, 1974).

4. Kevin Phillips, *The Politics of Rich and Poor* (New York: Random House, 1990).

5. David Riesman, et al., *The Lonely Crowd* (New Haven, CT: Yale University Press, 1950).

6. William H. Whyte, *The Organization Man* (New York: Simon and Schuster, 1956).

7. Vance Packard, *The Hidden Persuaders* (New York: D. McKay Co., 1957).

8. Michael Parenti, *Inventing Reality: Politics and the Mass Media* (New York: St. Martin's Press, 1986).

9. Abbie Hoffman with Jonathan Silvers, *Steal This Urine Test* (New York: Penguin Books, 1987), 142.

10. Ibid., p. 150.

11. Ibid., p. 144.

12. Abbie Hoffman, Jerry Rubin and Ed Sanders, *Vote* (New York: Warner Paperback Library, 1972), 105.

13. Hoffman, et al., *Steal This Urine Test*, p. 144.

14. Ibid., p. 150.

15. Hoffman, et al., *Vote*, p. 31.

16. Ibid., p. 31–32.

17. Ibid., p. 11.

18. Abbie Hoffman, *Steal This Book* (New York: Pirate Editions, 1971), v.

19. Hoffman, et al., *Vote*, p. 144.

20. Hoffman, *Steal this Book*, p. vi-vii, (emphasis ours).

21. Hoffman, et al., *Steal This Urine Test*, p. 2.

22. Ibid., p. 170–171.

23. Ibid., p. 159.

24. Abbie Hoffman, *Soon To Be a Major Motion Picture* (New York: Putnam Books, 1980), 113.

25. Ibid., p. 109.

26. Ibid., p. 230.

Part III. Standing on the Shoulders of Giants: Hoffman in an American Philosophical Context

1. Thomas Jefferson, *Writings* (New York: Literary Classics of the United States, 1984), 494.

2. Ibid., p. 880.

3. Thomas Jefferson, vol. X of *The Writings of Thomas Jefferson*, Paul Leicester Ford, ed. (New York: G.P. Putnam's Sons, 1899), 161.

4. John Dewey, *Freedom and Culture* (New York: G.P. Putnam's Sons, 1939), 129.

5. John Dewey, *Individualism Old and New* (New York: Capricorn Books, 1962), 61.

6. Ibid., p. 84

7. Amy Guttman, *Democratic Education* (Princeton: Princeton University Press, 1987), 13.

8. "Free" [Abbie Hoffman], *Revolution for the Hell of It* (New York: Dial Press, 1968), 167.

9. Ibid., p. 168.

10. See Theodore L. Becker and Richard Scarce, "Teledemocracy Emergent," in Brenda Dervin and Melvin Voigt (eds) *Progress in Communications Science* (Norwood, N.J.: Ablex, 1986); Christa Daryl Slaton, *The Televote Experiments: Citizen Participation in the Quantum Age* (New York: Praeger Publishers, 1992).

11. Erich Fromm, *The Sane Society* (Greenwich, CT: Fawcett Publications, 1955).

12. Hoffman, *Revolution for the Hell of It*, p. 168.

13. Abbie Hoffman with Jonathan Silvers, *Steal This Urine Test* (New York: Penguin Books, 1987), 146.

14. Hoffman, *Revolution for the Hell of It*, p. 167.

15. Abbie Hoffman, *The Best of Abbie Hoffman* (New York: Four Walls Eight Windows, 1989), 370.

16. Abbie Hoffman, *Soon to be a Major Motion Picture* (New York: Putnam Books, 1980), 107.

17. Hoffman, *The Best of Abbie Hoffman*, p. 374.

18. Jefferson, *Writings*, p. 882.

19. Ibid., p. 911.

20. Dewey, *Individualism Old and New*, p. 93.

21. Ibid., p. 114.

22. Merle Curti, *The Growth of American Thought* (New York: Harper & Row, 1964), 359. (Emphasis ours.)

23. Ralph Waldo Emerson, vol. 1 of *The Collected Works of Ralph Waldo Emerson* (Cambridge, Mass.: The Belknap Press of Harvard University Press, 1971), 156.

24. Milton Meltzer, *Thoreau: People, Principles, and Politics* (New York: Hill and Wang, 1963), ix.

25. Curti, *The Growth of American Thought.* p. 412.

26. Henry David Thoreau, *The Writings of Henry David Thoreau* (Boston and New York: Houghton Mifflin Co., 1906), 15.

27. Ibid., p. 387.

28. Abbie Hoffman, *Square Dancing in the Ice Age* (Boston: South End Press, 1982), x.

29. Hoffman, et al., *Steal This Urine Test*, p. 4.

30. Hoffman, *Soon to be a Major Motion Picture*, p. 297.

31. Ibid., p. 83.

32. Ibid., p. 249.

33. Ibid., p. 249.

34. Hoffman, et al., *Steal This Urine Test*, p. 249.

35. Ibid., p. 249.

36. Hoffman, *The Best of Abbie Hoffman*, p. 378.

37. Hoffman, *Revolution For the Hell of It*, p. 166.

38. Ibid., p. 114.

39. Ibid., p. 115.

40. Ibid., pp. 105–106.

41. Hoffman, *The Best of Abbie Hoffman*, p. 372.

42. Alvin Toffler is responsible for this phrase. See his *Future Shock* (New York: Random House, 1970).

43. Marshall McLuhan, *Understanding the Media* (New York: American Library, 1964), and *The Medium is the Massage* (New York: Random House, 1967).

44. Betty Friedan, *The Feminist Mystique* (New York: Norton, 1963).

45. James Lovelock, *Gaia: A New Look at Life on Earth* (New York: Oxford University Press, 1979).

46. Hoffman, *Square Dancing in the Ice Age*, p. 81.

47. Jon Kalish, "No-Nuke Nation," an interview with Abbie Hoffman, *The Soho News*, 17 May 1979.

48. Hoffman, *Soon to be a Major Motion Picture*, p. 281.

49. Ibid., p. 281.

50. Hoffman, *The Best of Abbie Hoffman*, p. 415–416.

51. Ibid., p. 416.

52. Abbie Hoffman, _Woodstock Nation_ (New York: Vintage Books, 1969), 105.

53. Hoffman, _The Best of Abbie Hoffman_, p. 379.

54. Hoffman, _Soon to be a Major Motion Picture_, p. 106.

55. For an exceptional discussion of "relational rights" see Gus di Zerega, "Green Politics and Post-Modern Liberalism," _Critical Review_ (Spring 1987): 17–41; also, Gus di Zerega, "Integrating Quantum Theory with Post-Modern Political Thought and Action, in Theodore L. Becker, _Quantum Politics_ (New York: Praeger Publishers, 1991).

Index

About the Authors

THEODORE L. BECKER's father was a prominent lawyer and oft-defeated Republican politician in the city of Newark, New Jersey, during the 1930s and 1940s. He wanted his son to inherit his law practice, but avoid practicing politics. After finishing his law degree at Rutgers Law School, the son decided to avoid practicing law and, instead, study, teach and write about politics. So, he went to Northwestern and earned a Ph.D. in political science. Since then, Ted Becker has taught at several colleges and universities in the United States (Oakland University, Wayne State, New York University, CCNY, Brooklyn College, Cal State at Los Angeles, San Diego State) and one abroad (Victoria University in New Zealand). He was also the chairman of the departments of political science at the University of Hawaii and at Auburn University (where he is now). In addition, he has written nine other books including studies on political trials, government lawlessness, American government and quantum politics. At this point in his life, he believes that although his late mother and father would still want him to be a practicing attorney, they would finally be pleased with the path he chose.

ANTHONY L. DODSON was born in Ankara, Turkey, where his father was a captain in the United States Army and his mother was a school teacher. Growing up in Illinois, he was strongly influenced by the turbulence of the 1960s and 1970s. Thereafter, he spent his post-high school years travelling throughout the South and settled for some time in Mobile, Alabama, where he tended bar, did a lot of fishing, and earned his B.A. from the University of South Alabama. He is presently completing his master's degree at Auburn University and intends to finish up a Ph.D. in political science at the University of Nebraska. After that he'd like to settle somewhere in the Southeast to teach, write, and LIVE THIS BOOK!